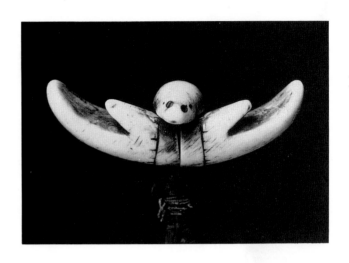

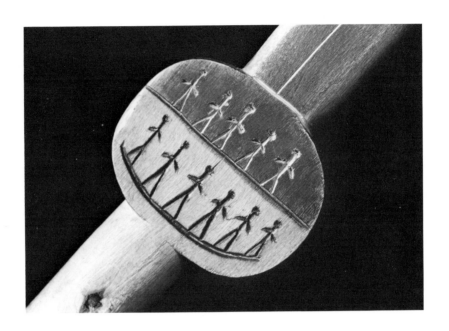

Julie Cruikshank

Reading Voices
Dän Dhá Ts'edenintth'é
Oral and Written Interpretations

of the Yukon's Past

Douglas & McIntyre
Vancouver/Toronto

Copyright © 1991 Julie Cruikshank

All rights are reserved. No part of this book may be reproduced or transmitted in any form or by any means without permission in writing from the publisher, except by a reviewer, who may quote brief passages in a review.

Douglas & McIntyre Ltd.
1615 Venables Street
Vancouver, British Columbia
V5L 2H1

Published with assistance from the Yukon Department of Education.

This book was edited and designed for Douglas & McIntyre by Robert Bringhurst Ltd. The typefaces used are Sabon, designed by Jan Tschichold; Syntax, designed by Hans Eduard Meier; and Zapf International, designed by Hermann Zapf.

Typesetting and page imposition by The Typeworks, Vancouver. Cartography by Angus Weller. Printing and binding by Everbest Printing, Hong Kong.

Canadian Cataloguing in Publication Data:

Cruikshank, Julie.
   Dän Dhá Ts'edenintth'é = Reading voices

   Includes bibliographical references and index.
   ISBN 0-88894-728-3

1 Indians of North America – Yukon
   Territory – History.
2 Yukon Territory – History.
3 Oral history.
I Title.
II Title: Reading voices.

   E78.Y8C78 1991   971.9′1004972
   C91-091219-X

The Yukon Archives photos reproduced in this book come from the following collections: J. A. Phelps (p 28), Beatty (pp 58, 98), Claude Tidd (p 70 top), Their Own Yukon (pp 70 bottom, 76, 95 bottom), Van Bibber (p 71), NMC (p 97), Wm Geddes (p 106 bottom), Byers (p 111), Skookum Jim Oral History Project (p 120), Canadian Bank of Commerce Collection (p 123).

Contents

LIST OF MAPS

Introduction

M OST BOOKS are the product of the work, efforts, and ideas of many people. This is especially true of *Reading Voices/Dän Dhá Ts'edenintth'é.* It originated from a growing concern among Yukon educators that many voices have been left out of written Yukon history. It reflects a conviction that high school students need to hear those voices – particularly the voices of the Yukon's First Nations – when they read about the Yukon's past.

It is important to outline briefly how this book came to be written. Sharon Jacobs and Clara Schinkel from the Council for Yukon Indians, Bob Sharp at the Department of Education, and Ken Taylor with the Yukon Teachers' Association developed a way to include these missing voices. All four have long-term experience working in Yukon schools. They established a working committee representing each of their organizations. They asked me to write the book because I brought to the process the expertise of my own teachers – Mrs Angela Sidney, Mrs Kitty Smith, Mrs Annie Ned, Mrs Rachel Dawson, Johnny Johns, John Joe, George Dawson and others who have taught me during the last twenty years. As each chapter was written, the committee met with me to review and discuss the result, and their suggestions were woven into the manuscript.

When a draft was completed, the committee organized a weekend workshop with six elders who agreed to discuss the manuscript. They came from different parts of the Yukon and have all been involved in school programs themselves, as language instructors, as school committee members, as cultural consultants, as storytellers. Robert Bruce, born in 1913, travelled from Old Crow for the meetings: he was able to talk about the eight years he spent in Carcross Residential School as a child and how much he had to relearn about life on the land when he returned to Old Crow at the age of sixteen. Mrs Helen Buyck has been an active member of the Mayo band council and the Mayo school committee as well as a Native language instructor. She consistently brought a northern Yukon perspective to our discussions and it was she who provided the book's title in the Northern Tutchone language. Mrs Clara Donnessy came from Watson Lake and talked about her childhood growing up in the Dease and Liard Rivers, and how life changed after the construction of the Alaska Highway. Percy Henry, who teaches the Han language to adult classes, discussed his youth as a trapper on the Wind and Blackstone Rivers, his adult years working on the riverboats, and his years of experience as chief of the people living at Dawson City. Mrs Annie Ned and Mrs Angela Sidney, both major contributors to this book, also attended the workshop. Their voices are among those frequently heard on the following pages.

Two themes emerged from these discussions. First, elders talked about the continuing importance of *words*. They insist that people still make use of longstanding traditions to think about life. Oral tradition does not simply tell us about the past; it continues to provide guidelines for the present and to lay a foundation for thinking about the future. Secondly, elders pointed to the continuing importance of *things* – the visible, material heritage that is steadily vanishing over time. They talked about the traps, the snares, the many strategies people used to provide a life based on fishing, hunting and trapping. They spoke about the ceremonial clothing, the decorated tools, the small works of art that were part of daily life. These, they say, provide the concrete examples they should be able to point to when they try to teach younger people about how life used to be conducted. Both words and things have an ongoing role in reproducing an understanding of the past.

This volume covers the period before the twentieth century. It raises a series of questions that can be asked at a community level rather than presuming to give a set of self-contained answers. The concern here is less with determining "truth value" or with "getting the facts straight" than with asking how our ideas about "truth" and "facts" are constructed in the first place. Understanding perspectives from different cultural traditions enlarges our understanding of the past.

A book inevitably reflects the experiences of the person who actually writes it. While I bring particular questions to research, my perspective inevitably reflects what I have learned from my teachers, most of whom are from the southern Yukon, and most of whom are women. Unless otherwise stated, their words cited in the book come from conversations we have had over twenty years. Elders from other parts of the Yukon who met at our workshop agree that while the examples in this book are specific, the questions should be asked of men as well as of women, and in northern communities as well as those in the southern Yukon. They suggest that the testimonies included in this book should send readers out to other elders.

Two stylistic issues should be mentioned. The term "elder" is used in everyday discussion in the Yukon now and appears frequently in the following pages. The term has no direct parallel in indigenous languages – the closest approximation being, for example, *hudé hudän* in the Tutchone language, or *kwäday kwadän* in Southern Tutchone, meaning "long ago people." An English term was needed that conveys the same sense of respect, and for that purpose "elder" is now used in the Yukon, as elsewhere in Canada. It has been the custom in the Yukon to capitalize the word "Elder," but it is really a term with roots in oral tradition. In this book we follow the conventions of written English and do not capitalize except in special circumstances.

Readers will also notice that I use "Mrs" when referring to women elders – Mrs Sidney, Mrs Smith, Mrs Ned – while omitting "Mr" for men like Johnny Johns, George Dawson, John Joe. Both elders and young people agree that this convention dates to the introduction of the English language to the Yukon and has long been followed by both

men and women to refer to their elders when the names are given in English.

My personal thanks go to several friends whose contribution occurred outside the official process – Carol Geddes, who continues to contribute enormously to my understanding of southern Yukon society; Virginia Appell, whose insightful editorial comments on early drafts of the manuscript were invaluable; Jeannie Maddison, who housed me while I was writing a final draft. My thanks, too, to John Ritter, Gertie Tom, Margaret Workman and the staff of the Yukon Native Language Centre for their patient help with translations and with questions about Native languages. I am also grateful to Robin Armour, Helen Dobrowolsky, Linda Johnson and the staff of the Yukon Archives for their help with photographs, and to Garry Clarke for his willingness to read and comment critically on various versions of the manuscript. It has been a great pleasure to work with Robert Bringhurst, the editor and designer of this book, and I thank him especially for showing me how to use words to say what I mean in a cleaner, clearer style.

J.C.

Kitty Smith (c. 1890 – 1989) was born somewhere near the mouth of the Álsek River. She was raised on the upper Alsek near the old village of Dalton Post. Her mother, *Tatl'èrma,* was from Marsh Lake, while her father, *Tàkàtà,* had coastal Tlingit ancestors. Mrs Smith's mother died when she was very young and she was raised by her father's people on the Alsek and Tatshenshini river system. There she learned songs, stories and customs from the southwest Yukon. As an adult, she married Billy Smith, and the couple settled some distance east of where she grew up, in her "mother's country," at Robinson. In this area, near Marsh Lake and Carcross, she learned traditions quite different from those of her father's people. Throughout her life, Mrs Smith has always considered storytelling a crucial way of acquiring knowledge. Many of her stories were published during her lifetime, in booklets issued by the Council for Yukon Indians. *Photo by Jim Robb, 1988.*

Oral and Written Interpretations of the Past 1

THE AREA now known as the Yukon Territory has a history as ancient as the earth itself. There are many narratives about how the world began – some told by scientists, some by historians and some by First Peoples whose oral traditions address similar questions. The stories told by elders and those told by scientists and historians have developed differently and depend on different sources, but both attempt to interpret how things came to be the way they are. These different interpretations of the past give us a sense of the richness of human history in the Yukon, though the explanations cannot easily be compared.

Inquiries about the past lead us to ask even more basic questions. How do we know what we know? What kinds of evidence do we use? What is "evidence" anyway? How is our understanding of the world constructed in the first place? These are some of the questions we will explore in the following pages. In this chapter we look at how *oral tradition* presents one way of interpreting Yukon landscape, climate and ecology. In the next chapter we will pay attention to how the scientific tradition adds to our understanding of these same topics. In later chapters we look at the contribution of written history.

We may talk about oral and written traditions as though they are passed on independently. In our own lives, though, most of us combine what we learn in books with what we learn by word of mouth. In the Yukon especially, we have opportunities to learn about the world from both written and oral sources. In the words of elder Mrs Kitty Smith: "Well, my grandchild is six years old now. She's going to start school pretty soon now. Pretty soon, paper's going to talk to her." But if she is lucky, the oral tradition is going to keep talking to her as well.

Storytelling may be the oldest of the arts. We know that every culture on earth has passed essential ideas from one generation to the next by word of mouth. But in many parts of the world, the power of the written word has displaced the power of the spoken word. In the Yukon, we are fortunate to have elders who are still able and willing to teach younger people.

Indigenous knowledge and the European scientific tradition present very different models for thinking about the world. For example, a scientist may link information about any point on the earth's surface to a series of numbers giving its *longitude*, its *latitude* and its *altitude*. To people who live there, that place may have further dimensions. Elders often give a very different picture of landscape than scientists do. They tell stories of how a particular place came to be, the events that happened there in the distant past when animals and humans could still

A long time ago all the world was water. Crow saw that Sea Lion owned the only island in the world. The rest was water. Sea Lion is the only one with land. The whole place was ocean.

Crow is resting on a piece of log. He's tired. He sees Sea Lion with that little island just for himself. He wants land too.

So he stole that Sea Lion's kid.

"Give me back that kid," said Sea Lion.

"Give me some beach, some sand," says Crow. So Sea Lion gave him sand. You know how sand in water floats? Crow threw that sand around the ocean.

"Be world!" he tells it. And it became the world.
– Angela Sidney, *My Stories Are My Wealth*, p 3

We are storytelling animals, and cannot bear to acknowledge the ordinariness of our daily lives (and even of most events that, in retrospect, seem crucial to our fortunes and our history). We therefore retell actual events as stories with moral messages, embodying a few limited themes that narrators through the ages have cultivated for their power to interest and instruct.
– Stephen Jay Gould, *Wonderful Life: The Burgess Shale and the Nature of History*, p 70

Note: All books quoted or mentioned in the text are listed in the bibliography, page 152.

While it may seem contradictory to go to books for examples of oral tradition, Yukon elders recognize the power of the written word and have begun recording their stories in a form that can be read. Reading stories is no substitute for hearing them told. Whenever possible, you should listen to elders tell stories; however, reading them can prepare you to listen for different themes. See *John Fredson Edward Sapir Hàa Googwandak;* Angela Sidney, Kitty Smith and Rachel Dawson, *My Stories Are My Wealth;* Angela Sidney, *Tagish Tlaagú;* Kitty Smith, *Nindal Kwädindür.* For a guide to themes in these latter three booklets, see *When the World Began* by Julie Cruikshank.

talk to one another, and the events that have occurred there in historical times. They locate the place not by means of numbers on a grid, but by means of a narrative, a story. And that story may flow into other stories, like a trail or a stream.

In the oral tradition, names instead of numbers are used for locating one place in relation to another. When Angela Sidney talks about Tagish Lake, she tells how Fox named the streams, the islands, the points of land at the beginning of time. She locates the places by tracing Fox's journey:

One time Fox came to people at the head of Tagish River.
They call that Taagish T'óo'e' *in Tagish language,*
Taagish Héeni *in Tlingit.*
"My brother-in-law," he said.
He happened to be Crow and he's speaking to his Wolf.
"From here, you go.
You get down the lake from here.
You go to that K'aa' Deitl'óoní – *that means "where arrows are tied up in a bundle."*
That's Tagish language. Tlingit is Chooneit Wusi.axu Yé.
Now they call it "Frying Pan Island" because it's sometimes joined to the shore.
It's across from Ten Mile, Tsuxx'aayí.
"Put bait in the water.
From here on, you go. . . ."

They call that mountain behind that place K'aa' Deitl'óoní Dzéłe'.
Chooneit Shaayí, *Tlingit way.*

He's the one, Fox, gave Indian names to all those points on Tagish Lake.
They still use them, Indian way.

Oral narratives from the Yukon may sound more like literature than science. In the European educational system, a sharp distinction has been made for several hundred years between "arts" (including language, literature, history) and "sciences" (including mathematics, physics, chemistry). But Europeans have not always organized their knowledge in this way, and to people of other cultures the distinction can seem quite pointless and artificial.

Oral and scientific traditions not only speak from different perspectives; they are passed along in different ways. Oral traditions survive by repeated retellings, and each narrative contains more than one message. The listener is part of the storytelling event too, and is expected to think about and interpret the messages in the story. A good listener will bring different life experiences to the story each time he or she hears it and will learn different things each time. Oral tradition is like a prism which becomes richer as we improve our ability to view it from a variety of angles. It does not try to spell out everything one needs to know, but rather to make the listener think about ordinary experiences in new ways.

Scientific information is usually circulated in written form, in journals or in books. Once accounts are written down they can be stored unchanged. Unless they are physically destroyed, they can be reread and inspected by anyone who goes to a library to read them. Scientific accounts are always open to further tests and different interpretations by other scientists, who may carry the research in new directions. But when a complex experiment has been checked and published, it is often not repeated. The results alone are retained.

In the realm of history too, oral traditions have much to teach us. Many early written accounts about Yukon life come from short-term visitors who arrived during the gold rush, just before the twentieth century. Their observations tell us a good deal about prospectors' lives, but less about the aboriginal people who had always lived in the area. Oral traditions about the same events often present a very different picture.

Like the historical and scientific traditions, the oral tradition also has its favorite themes. The stories of Yukon elders explore how the world began, how it was transformed to its present state, how the balance between animals and humans is maintained.

Throughout North America, Native peoples tell how the world as we understand it was originally set in order by a Creator/Trickster/Transformer. In the Yukon, Crow has this role. He is sometimes a wise all-knowing being, sometimes a ridiculous fool, sometimes a danger to himself and others, and his very human characteristics give rise to a marvellous oral literature about his exploits. Ask an elder to tell you about Crow and you will hear a seemingly endless range of narratives. Older people say that it used to take days for a good storyteller to tell about all of Crow's adventures. Other Yukon narratives tell how the world was transformed from a state when animals and humans were enemies to a point where they achieved balance. Animal Mother, Beaverman, and the Two Smart Brothers each played a part in making the world safe for humans. Still other stories tell about how humans and animals continue to share the world, and how humans must be reprimanded periodically, when their self-centred arrogance threatens all living beings.

Mythology differs from science, but both are organized systems of knowledge based on close study of the environment. Both systems take many years to learn, and both are perpetually open and incomplete. Until recently, every Yukon child learned about the world by observation and through oral instruction. Adults guided the discoveries of children with cycles of stories about relations between animals and people. A young person might learn a range of strategies for coping with a difficult problem by listening to how the main character in a story handled that problem. Practical information about aspects of bush life, like snaring, trapping, locating berry grounds, or building a fire in difficult circumstances, is often included in longer stories. With the help of narratives, adults taught youngsters what to observe and how to understand and interpret the details of the world around them.

Edwin Scurvey once explained,

If I ever get stuck in the bush, I wouldn't have any trouble. I'd just remember what Äsùya did when he was travelling around and I'd know what to do. You follow that story and it tells you everything you need to know. That's how they used to teach us when we were kids.

To learn more about Crow, see *My Stories Are My Wealth*, pp 1–21; *Tagish Tlaagú*, pp 1–15; and *When the World Began*, pp 16–17 & 41–42. For stories about Animal Mother, Beaverman and the Two Smart Brothers, see *My Stories Are My Wealth*, pp 22–44 & 85–92, and *When the World Began*, pp 42–44.

Stories about the consequences of human arrogance include Angela Sidney's narratives "The Boy Who Stayed with Fish" and "The Man Who Stayed with Groundhog Woman" in *My Stories Are My Wealth*. See also *When the World Began*, p 44.

Kitty Smith

That Crow, he's like God.
This is how he made the world.
Long time ago, animals were all people.
This is before they had light.
One time they were all out fishing.
Fox and Bear were fishing there – they talk like person.
Crow comes up.

"Caw! You sleep, you fellows.
If I make daylight, you're going to be scared," he said.
Crow says that. He's really an Indian, though.

People say, "You know that man who's got it? Sun?
That's his daughter's place in there.
He keeps her there, just like old time.
You can't get that kind," they told him.

That big poplar tree right there is rotten inside.
He takes that inside off, throws it beside there.
He throws that tree in the lake, goes in the lake.
He doesn't know where he's going.
He can't die, that Crow, can't get killed.

"That man where he stays, he's got that sun,
that's the place I want it.
I want my boat landed there."
That's what he said.
He made a song about that. I know that song too.

Nighttime.
Gee, big house there.
Looks just like it's got a light on.

He got out, walked around.
He sees where that big water runs down.
He just thinks. . . .
He turns himself into a little dirt,
puts himself right there.
"I wish she wants to get water."
He wants to see that house now.
"I wish that woman wants to drink water."

That lady comes to get water.
Just like a dish, that pot.
He goes into that pot, goes in like a little dirt.
He stays there.
She goes in.

Gee, it shines, that house!
Light in there. Big one! Two.
Right there and right there.
That's where he throws that light.

He thinks, "What am I going to do?"
That girl is a young girl.
What do you think he did? He went in that cup!
That girl started to drink the water and she swallowed him down!

Just in two weeks, her stomach got big, that girl.
No man here – nothing!
Her mother tells her husband,
"Our girl is going to have a baby.
Where does he come from, that baby?"

"I don't know," he said.

Just one month now she starts to have that baby, gets sick.
He's rich man, that man, that Daddy.
Puts everything underneath.
That baby is going to be born on top!

Crow thinks, "I'm going to be born-on-top baby.
I wish they would put some grass under me."
That's what he thinks. He thinks for that lady's nurse,
"Get grass, get grass."

That girl is getting tired now.
That lady says,
"I'm going to get that grass. Good one.
I'm going to fix it underneath."
She did it just right then.
It's soft, just like a feather pillow. He's born there.
It's cold. Indian climate is cold, see?

Little boy.
Ah, gee, he sees his grandma.
"Ah, my little grandchild!"

He did that [winked] with his eye. Bad kid!
"Why did he do that?" she asks her husband.
"He did that with his eye."

"I guess he's playing with you," he told her.
"You see now?
Hi, little baby!
You're going to laugh, you," he told him.

Just in one week, he started to walk. In two weeks, he's that big.
He runs around.
Up there are those big ones, the moon and the sun.
Those are the ones he's going to throw.

He starts to cry for that moon.

"Take it down, Momma, I want to play with it."

His grandpa said,
"I don't want that baby to cry.
Take it off. Let him play with it. He can't lose it."

He roll it around, I don't know where he put it.
Maybe he swallowed it, I don't know, but he got it!
They look around all over. Lost!
Just that old sun is there now.

After about one week, he started to cry.
He cried and cried.
He's got that moon though. Someplace he's got it.
He cried and cried and his eyes just about slipped out!

His grandpa said, "Take it off.
I don't like my grandchild's eyes that way."

He played around.
He's going to get away now with that one.
They open someplace when that house is hot.
They got a lady working there, you know.

"Say, lady," he tells her, "Open that. It's too hot."

"You feel hot?"

"Yes," he says.

She opens it.
He's going to get out that way.
They should put that sun away now!

Gone!

"Where's that little kid?"

Some place he falls down, they think.

Crow is thinking about his boat, rotten one.
Just uses it for a boat. He's going to go in it soon.
"I want to be at that fishing place, down the bay," he said.
Don't know how long he stayed in that boat.
"Whew, whew," he paddles.

There's that place. They're fishing yet!

"I'm going to make daylight, you people.
Just quiet now," he said.

"Aw, you got no light, you got no sun," they tell him.
He's got them now!

"What do you think I'm going to do?
The best way, I'm going to throw it in the sky.
It's going to stay there."

He throws that moon the first time.
"Stay there for good," he said.
After that, he pulled out that sun.
He threw it.

Everything go into the water.
Just one little boy, one little girl they still walk on four hands.
They want to walk that way and he grabs them.

"You're going to walk on two feet.
You're not going to walk on four feet.
I've got two feet, I walk," he said.
He grabbed those kids, one little girl, one little boy.

"I'm going to raise you," he said.
"Sun up there now, daylight now."

Some of them go into the water,
some of them go into the woods.
They run away.

Two kids only, he saved, one little girl and one little boy.
You're going to have twelve kids," he told them, that girl,
"This one is going to marry you.
You are going to have two feet.
You're not going to walk like that.
Your hair is going to be this way, and your hands."
He showed them.

"No more.
That sun is going to stay for good.
This ground turns, but that sun stays in one place.
Moon same too.
He don't move, he just stays there."
That's what he said, that Crow.

Those kids, he made them grow.
In the morning, he made them get up, those kids.
He rubs their backs to make them grow. Funny, eh?

Then he gets grub for them.
"What grub am I going to get?" he said.
He brought them grub, gave them some kind of fish.

That Crow, he does everything, teaches everything.
Which way they're going to kill fish, he teaches.
Fish trap, he makes it. Hook he makes it.
My grandson read that Bible for me.
Pretty near the same, I think.
He's Jesus, I guess. God maybe.

Attractions and Limitations of Oral Tradition

We learn from Grandma, Grandpa,
what they do, and they explain to us.
I think everybody knows that, but I
know what they say. . . . Just like
you're learning things. Just like
you're going to school. They tell
stories to make your mind strong.
– Mrs Annie Ned, elder

I feel like I was planted here like a
forest tree and raised here, not going
nowhere and just sitting like a plant
and getting old, and I know I'm
going to die here. I'm not going to
die somewhere else.
– Mrs Lena Johnson, elder, speaking to
the Alaska Highway Pipeline Inquiry at
Burwash Landing, 1977

STORIES ENDURE. A major attraction of oral tradition is that the narratives persist. Many aspects of Inland Tlingit and Northern Athapaskan life have changed enormously during the last century. The fur trade, the gold rush, the various dislocations associated with missionary activity, schools and industrial development have all brought radical changes to the First Peoples of the Yukon. Yet oral traditions survive and continue to have meaning in the contemporary lives of adults who tell and hear them. In fact, stories recorded a century ago, by visitors who believed they were hearing them from the last elders who knew them, are *still* told by Athapaskan and Tlingit elders in the 1990s.

Oral narratives include historical events. Because oral traditions are never fixed or static, historical events are often woven into existing stories. Narratives deal with ancient themes, like creation, but they include references to changes in animal populations, to the coming of first whites, and to the gold rush. They also incorporate observations about weather and about cataclysmic events like glacial surges and volcanic eruptions. And traditional narratives don't just describe events: they also offer explanations of *why* they occurred.

Observations are made over a lifetime. Hunting peoples carefully study animal and plant life cycles, topography, seasonal changes and mineral resources. Elders speaking about landscape, climate and ecological changes are usually basing their observations on a lifetime of experience. In contrast, because much scientific research in the north is university-based, it is organized around short summer field seasons. The long-term observations included in oral accounts provide important perspectives on the questions scientists are studying.

It's important to get the words right. The ability to create, in words, a situation for a listener who might have to experience it sometime in the future is important. It is the reason elders like Mrs Annie Ned emphasize the importance of telling the stories accurately, or in her own words, the importance of "getting the words right." Eventually, everyone has to rely on lessons learned orally.

While there is much to be learned from oral narrative, there are also some limitations to keep in mind. It is never simple to interpret ideas across cultural boundaries. Whenever a story seems simple, we should suspect that we do not really understand it.

Young people living in Yukon communities in the 1990s have different experiences from those of elder storytellers, so sometimes they find it hard to understand all the details in the stories. In earlier times, everyone who heard a story would share certain understandings of the world. Elders are often extremely generous in assuming that their listeners are familiar with traditions they themselves learned as children. Consequently, they may begin telling a story without filling in the background every listener needs to know.

Language is another critical issue. Narratives told in an Athapaskan language or Tlingit and then translated into English usually lose a lot in the process. During the last thirty or forty years, many Native

Yukon children have grown up speaking English as their first language. English is a language with many more nouns than Athapaskan languages, but Athapaskan languages have a much richer system of verbs. This poses serious problems for adequately expressing ideas from one language in another. Elders know this, yet their commitment to teaching leads them to tell stories willingly in whatever language is clearest for their listeners.

The English language pays particular attention to time, space, and quantity; speakers of Athapaskan and Tlingit languages may choose to pay attention to form and shape, and to other characteristics. For example, Athapaskan speakers use different verb stems to show whether things are animate or inanimate, rigid or flexible, moving or still, contained or uncontained. Athapaskan languages also express directions, distance and the relative position of things differently from English. In relation to a river, for instance, verbs can be modified to distinguish movement upriver, across the river, into the river. Students of oral traditions should recognize that such difficulties exist and be prepared to try to understand them.

Literary style is something schools teach us to think about in English classes, but we should be aware that each cultural tradition has its own literary style, metaphors and symbols. Narrative traditions vary, even within the Yukon. Sometimes an elder will use images that seem complicated to outsiders but have clear, shared meanings for people within the narrator's community. Like all literature, oral narratives may seek to transform rather than accurately reflect life, and this poses problems for people trying to learn details about historical events. Many of these literary devices are independent of language. Older storytellers bring the same range of literary skills – including allusion, figurative and symbolic speech – to storytelling even when they tell their stories in English.

In the next chapter, we turn to look at some of the knowledge scientists contribute to our understanding of the Yukon's place in the earth's history, climate and ecology. In many cases, elders talk about the same issues that concern scientists. This gives us an opportunity to see how two quite different perspectives – oral tradition and scientific research – provide us with a more complete sense of the Yukon's past than either would alone.

Narratives told by Native Yukon elders were written down in 1883 by a German ethnographer named Aurel Krause; by the French priest Emile Petitot in 1886; in 1909 by an American anthropologist named John Swanton; and in 1917 by James Teit, a Scotsman who recorded orally narrated accounts throughout interior British Columbia. Each of these men believed he was recording stories with the last elderly tellers in the community; yet the same narratives are told today by Mrs Angela Sidney, by Mrs Kitty Smith, by Mrs Annie Ned and by many other Yukon elders. For narratives that will sound familiar in Yukon communities, see Aurel Krause, *The Tlingit Indians* (p 197); Emile Petitot in Habgood's "Indian Legends of Northwestern Canada"; John Swanton, *Tlingit Myths and Texts;* and James Teit, "Kaska Tales."

Stories and names anchor people to place, but so do songs. When Mrs Annie Ned travels along the Alaska Highway, she names the hills, the rivers, the valleys that have been her home. She also sings the songs she and others have made. Sometimes she says, "You don't know this place so I'll sing it for you." She sings this song, for instance, as we drive past Dezadeash Lake or *Titl'at*. It was sung by Casey Fred once when his girlfriend was at one end of the lake and he was at the other. The wind came up, making it unsafe to cross the water, but he could see her fire, so he sang:

Jeneda	*nerts'eni*	*kwäna* [*no-a*]	*Titl'at*
she feels bad	they say of you	it happened at the same time	Dezadeash Lake
kwäts'an	*ningha̧*	*kwädura*	*le-hi-e-haya*
from	over you	they make a story	
łutla	*na-*	*nets'eduni̧*	*no-a*
truly	(question)	are they telling	(question)
ningha̧	*kwädura*	*le-hi-a-haya* [*zu̧ą̧*]	
over you	they make a story		

They say that you are feeling badly at Dezadeash Lake.
Is this story they are telling about you really true?

The conventional European scale, with twelve semitones to the octave, is not capable of capturing all the intervals used in Athapaskan music. Even the term "scale" is troublesome, because it implies harmonic relationships that may not exist in Athapaskan music. Often songs drift upward in pitch as they are sung. However, when I sing her song back to her using these notes, Mrs Ned generously says that it is "pretty good" and that I should "just keep on trying." Mrs Gertie Tom helped to transcribe the words.

Je -ne -da nerts' - e - ni kwä - na Titl' - at kwäts' -an

nin - ghą kwä -du - ra le - hi - e - ha - ya

łu - tla - (a) na - nets' - e - du - nį no - a

nin - ghą kwä - du - ra le - hi - a - hay.

Je - ne - da nerts' - e - ni no - a Titl' - at kwäts'-an

nin - ghą kwä - du - ra le - hi - a - hay - ya

łu - tla - (a) na - nets' - e - du - nį no - a

nin - ghą kwä - du - ra zų - ą - a - hay

* The pitch of this syllable lies on the quarter tone midway between B and middle C.

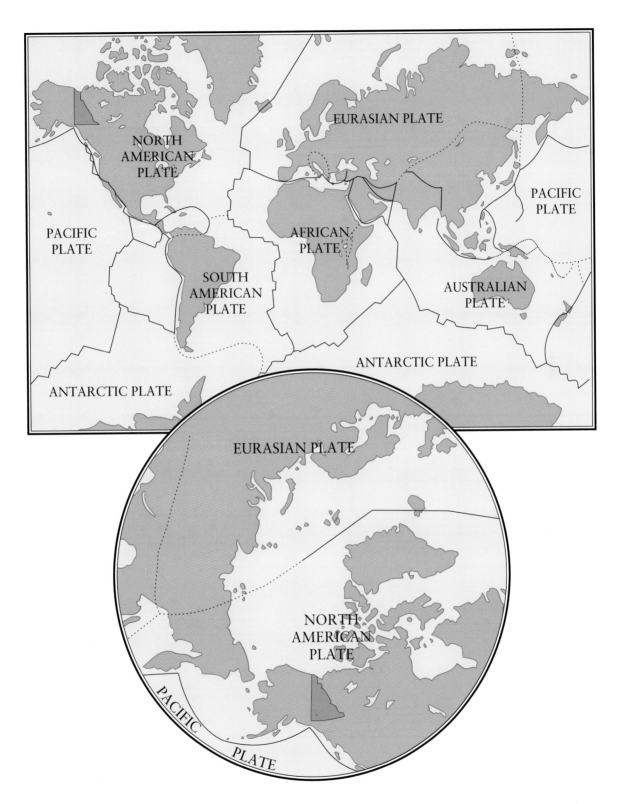

NORTH
AMERICAN
PLATE

EURASIAN PLATE

PACIFIC
PLATE

PACIFIC
PLATE

AFRICAN
PLATE

SOUTH
AMERICAN
PLATE

AUSTRALIAN
PLATE

ANTARCTIC PLATE

ANTARCTIC PLATE

EURASIAN PLATE

NORTH
AMERICAN
PLATE

PACIFIC
PLATE

The Earth's Major Tectonic Plates

Yukon Landscape, Climate and Ecology 2

HUMAN HISTORY is greatly influenced by the shape of the land and by the other living things that share the land. At the same time, the ways humans *think* about the land they inhabit have an enormous influence on the ways they behave toward it.

Our discussion of the Yukon landscape begins with reference to *physical features, climate, vegetation,* and *animals*. Each of these, in turn, has a history. Geological features have been changing for millions of years; so has climate. Changes in vegetation and in animal life also began in the distant past and continue today. If we look at each of these topics separately, we can investigate *processes* by which change occurs. As these processes become clearer, we can look at the *relationships* between landscape, climate, vegetation, and animals. We can begin to understand how they work together to create conditions for the development of human life, human culture and human history.

Physical Landscape

EARTH SCIENTISTS tell us that the earth has four main divisions: a solid inner core, a molten outer core, a thick rocky layer called the mantle, and a relatively thin outer crust (5–40 km thick) which is like a skin.

How old is this crust? The question takes us to an entirely different time scale, where even a million years is a short time. The oldest crust dates from the beginning of geologic history. This crust is made of enormous mosaic-like pieces – called tectonic plates – that carry the continents and the oceans we see on the earth's surface. These plates are like big rafts on an ocean of partly melted rock. The plates move very slowly – perhaps a centimetre or a few centimetres each year – but over millions of years they have wandered great distances. Sometimes they collide. Sometimes they break apart. Sometimes one plate slides under the edge of another. As the plates move, the surface of the land changes very slowly. Mountains are pushed up. Earthquakes occur. Volcanoes erupt. Then ice, water and wind shape the features we see.

North America has grown over billions of years as plates have pushed together, adding new parts to original plates. For example, the youngest mountains in the Yukon, the St Elias Mountains, are some of the highest in North America. They began to form millions of years ago when the Pacific plate collided with the Continental plate during the Mesozoic era. Ever so slowly, compression caused the land at the edge of the plates to buckle and fold into mountains. The collision of

Science is experiment: science is trying things. It is trying each possible alternative in turn, intelligently and systematically; and throwing away what won't work, and accepting what will, no matter how it goes against our prejudices. And what works adds one more piece to the slow, laborious . . . understanding of our world.
– Jacob Bronowski, *A Sense of the Future*, p 2

The attitude of an oral society toward speech is similar to the reverence of members of a literate society to the written word.
– Jan Vansina, "Once Upon a Time," p 442

There are two old ladies down below who look after the earth. One is supposed to be sleeping; the other one holds up the earth with a pole. When she shakes it, that's when there is supposed to be an earthquake. . . .
– Angela Sidney, *Tagish Tlaagú*, p 20

Geologists tell us that the earth is approximately 4.5 billion years old. They divide the geological time scale into *eras*, *periods*, and *epochs*.

The largest divisions, *eras*, are divided by major events. The boundary between Precambrian and Paleozoic eras – 570 million years ago – marks the first appearance of many-celled animals. The division between Paleozoic and Mesozoic – 225 million yeas ago – is a point at which the vast majority of marine species became extinct. The end of the Mesozoic – 65 million years ago – marks the extinction of the dinosaurs. The Cenozoic is the time when mammals began to develop.

We can get a clearer picture of what this means if we imagine the geological time scale speeded up so that it occurs over one calendar year. If the Precambrian era began on January 1st of our year, it would end on November 14th at the onset of the Paleozoic era. The Paleozoic would end on December 12th; the Mesozoic era would end on Christmas Day, December 25th. Our earliest hominid era ancestors from five million years ago would appear during the late evening of December 31st, and our own species, *homo sapiens*, would appear just minutes before midnight.

these plates resulted in the uplifting of the central Yukon Plateau, the dominant feature of the present Yukon Territory.

VOLCANOES

Many of the world's volcanoes are found where one tectonic plate is pressed against another or slides under the other. Volcanoes erupt when molten rock, called *magma*, rises from inside the earth. The plate movements that produce these eruptions also often cause earthquakes. Because of its position at the edge of the Continental plate, the Yukon has experienced volcanoes and earthquakes for millions of years.

One of the most famous eruptions occurred about 1200 years ago and blanketed much of the southern Yukon with ash. This eruption of the White River Volcano has been documented by scientists who are able to describe when it occurred and what its effects on human populations may have been.

In Alaska, more than 250 eruptions from 39 volcanoes have been reported in less than 200 years. Elders from the Yukon, Alaska and British Columbia can talk about eruptions that have occurred during their own lifetimes as well as ones they heard about from their elders. Ahtna people living on the Copper River in Alaska have traditions about volcanoes in the Wrangell Mountains. Tsimshian people in northern British Columbia tell about an eruption of Mount Edziza that happened 200 years ago. In the Yukon, Tommy McGinty heard from his parents and grandparents about an eruption of Volcano Mountain (called *Nelrúna* in Tutchone). He described this eruption in detail to geologists, who say that it occurred between 300 and 500 years ago and that McGinty's version is completely consistent with the scientific evidence.

Scientific observation of earthquakes in Alaska began in 1899. Since then, there have been at least two high-intensity quakes in the Shakwak Valley and Kluane Ranges and several in the northern Yukon and Mackenzie Valley. Because earthquake zones pose serious problems for construction projects, these earthquakes were of great interest in the mid-1970s when proposals were made to build a pipeline along either the Shakwak Valley or the Mackenzie Valley.

GEOLOGY AND LANDFORMS

Geologically, the Yukon is part of the *Canadian Cordillera* – the mountain system including both the Rocky Mountains and the Coast Mountains. The Cordillera runs from British Columbia and Alberta north through the Yukon, and northwest into Alaska. The geology of the Yukon shows a deeply etched pattern of mountains and valleys oriented along northwest/southeast lines. These parallel zones date from distinct geological time periods and are composed of different types of rocks.

The Selwyn and Ogilvie mountains, pushing up as folded sedimentary rocks, mark what is now the eastern boundary of the Yukon. They date from the *Paleozoic* and *Mesozoic* eras and are set off from

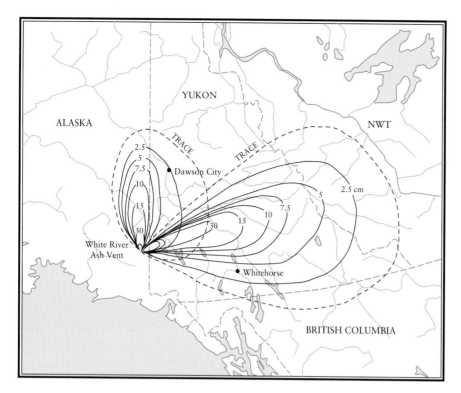

Ash from the White River volcanic eruption. Depths of the ash deposits are shown in centimetres. Scientific evidence suggests that the two lobes of ash were deposited several centuries apart. The northwestern lobe probably dates from about 1800 years ago and the larger eastern lobe from about 1200 years ago. *After Workman 1978.*

the rest of the Yukon by the Tintina Trench, a deep trench which drains the eastern lakes and streams via the Pelly River.

Dominating the Territory is the broad Yukon Plateau, averaging 1200 m above sea level. It is composed of sedimentary, metamorphic and volcanic rocks from *Precambrian* times and is crosscut by deep valleys and by the Yukon River.

In the southwest, the Plateau drops to a wide depression called the Shakwak Valley, which carries the Alaska Highway north of Whitehorse. That valley, in turn, rises sharply to the rugged St Elias range in the southwest corner of the Territory. These mountains are more recent than the Selwyn and Ogilvie ranges, dating in some places from the *Mesozoic* era and in others from the *Tertiary* period.

Such a dramatic landscape generates rich oral as well as scientific literature. Anyone fortunate enough to drive along the Alaska Highway or any other Yukon road with an elder will discover a different dimension to the Yukon landscape. For example, in *My Stories Are My Wealth* Angela Sidney names the four mountains around Carcross where Animal Mother hung her moosehide swing when she created animals at the beginning of time. Narratives like this one, anchored to geographical locations, give depth and richness to a landscape that Robert Service once mistakenly called "a land where the mountains are nameless."

Lakes like *Si män'* (Mush Lake) and *Täshäl män'* (Bates Lake), popular with modern canoers, have an alarming aspect in narratives told by Mrs Kitty Smith. She tells us that her grandfather once watched six caribou vanish as they were sucked into a whirlpool on Si män'. And a giant snake reportedly once lived in Täshäl män', emerging periodically to snatch game.

Geologists classify rocks into three types, depending on how they are formed. *Igneous* (or "fire-formed") rock occurs when magma cools and solidifies, either under the earth's surface or after a volcanic eruption. Granite, basalt and obsidian are all examples of igneous rocks found in the Yukon.

Sedimentary rock comes from fine sediments that are transported by wind, water and ice and then eventually deposited and compacted to become rock. Shale, sandstone and conglomerates are all examples of sedimentary rocks.

A third type of rock occurs when sedimentary or igneous rocks are subjected to intense pressure or heat which causes them to be physically changed into another kind of rock. Geologists refer to these as *metamorphic* (meaning "changed") rocks. Examples include gneiss, mica and marble.

See *Nindal Kwädindür*, pp 98–100.

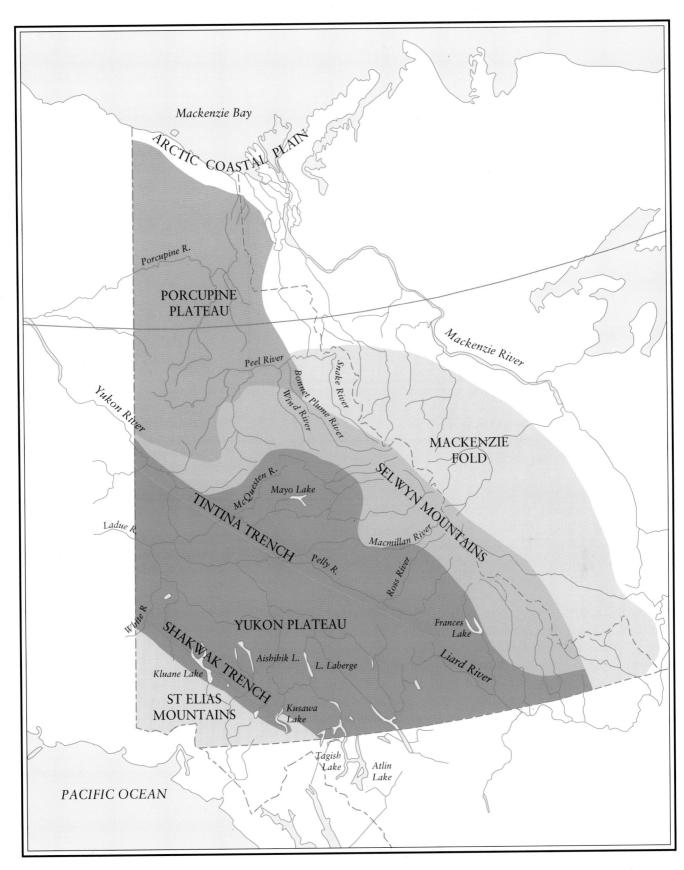

Mackenzie Bay

ARCTIC COASTAL PLAIN

Porcupine R.

PORCUPINE
PLATEAU

Mackenzie River

Peel River

Yukon River

Snake River

Bonnet Plume River

Wind River

MACKENZIE
FOLD

McQuesten R.

Mayo Lake

SELWYN MOUNTAINS

TINTINA TRENCH

Ladue R.

Macmillan River

Pelly R.

Ross River

White R.

YUKON PLATEAU

Frances
Lake

SHAKWAK TRENCH

Aishihik L.

L. Laberge

Liard River

Kluane Lake

ST ELIAS
MOUNTAINS

Kusawa
Lake

PACIFIC OCEAN

Tagish
Lake

Atlin
Lake

Physical Landscape of the Yukon, showing major mountain ranges, plateaux and valley trenches.

26

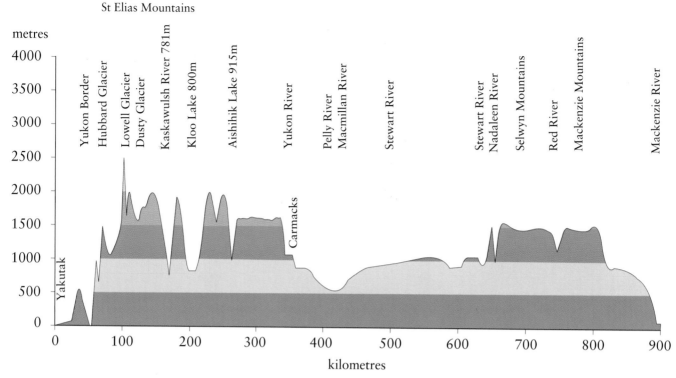

St Elias Mountains

metres

Yakutak

Yukon Border
Hubbard Glacier
Lowell Glacier
Dusty Glacier
Kaskawulsh River 781m
Kloo Lake 800m
Aishihik Lake 915m
Yukon River
Carmacks
Pelly River
Macmillan River
Stewart River
Stewart River
Nadaleen River
Selwyn Mountains
Red River
Mackenzie Mountains
Mackenzie River

kilometres

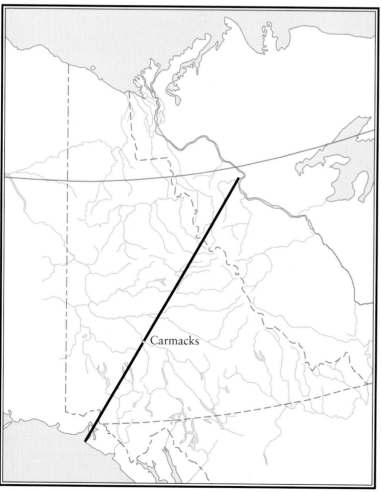

Carmacks

Yukon landscape in cross-section. Much of the Yukon is relatively high plateau land. The profile above shows the changes in elevation moving inland along a straight line from Yakutat through Carmacks to the Mackenzie River. Several peaks in the St Elias Mountains range up to 4000 m in altitude, but the highest point encountered along this particular line is only 2500 m. The line crosses the Shakwak Trench at Kloo Lake and the Yukon Plateau from Aishihik to Carmacks. It crosses the Tintina Trench near the confluence of the Pelly and Macmillan rivers. Then it crosses the Stewart River twice before entering the Mackenzie Mountains. *Note that the vertical scale is exaggerated almost 100 times in relation to the horizontal scale.*

Joe Ladue (on right) in 1942. *Yukon Archives photo.*

Yukon mountains and rocks come from each of the geological eras. The oldest known rocks in the world, four billion years old, were recently discovered near Great Slave Lake in the Northwest Territories.

In her book *Èkeyi: Gyò Cho Chú*, Gertie Tom tells us that a mountain just east of Teslin River, called "Sawtooth Range" in English, has a more vivid Tutchone name: *Ètsum Chíntth'ān Ddhāl*, "my grandmother's backbone mountain."

Aboriginal peoples have traditionally made detailed observations about geology, too. Often their willingness to share this information with outsiders has led to results they could not have anticipated. Stories about native copper in the White River area inspired early prospecting expeditions, and it was a Tagish man, Skookum Jim, who located the placer gold that led to the Klondike gold rush. (Oral traditions about this event are discussed in Chapter 7.) Joe Ladue, a Tutchone man, helped make the find that resulted in construction of a lead-zinc mine at Faro. The asbestos mine operating at Clinton Creek in the 1960s was built following the identification of asbestos near there by George Wood, a Han speaker.

Athapaskan place names themselves often encode precise information about geology and land forms. Place names in Athapaskan languages tell of the presence of obsidian in the Aishihik Valley, copper near the White River, red ochre on the Nisling and Donjek rivers, and flint at several places on Kluane Lake. The Tutchone name for Mendocina Creek, *Tthekál Chú*, refers to the thinly split rocks, *tthekál*, that are found there and are useful for tanning skins. The Tlingit name Angela Sidney gives for one of the mountains in the Animal Mother story, *Takaadí T'ooch'*, refers not merely to color but to an actual source of charcoal. A point of land at the north end of Marsh Lake is named *Mbésh Ta'áy*, "where the knife edge extends out" (Tagish), and *Lítaa Yak'áts'i Shaa*, "knife edge mountain" (Tlingit), because as one travels north by boat on Marsh Lake, it appears to rest against the water like the edge of a knife.

ANIMAL MOTHER'S MOUNTAINS

Angela Sidney

After those animals were born,
she made a big swing for them, a trampoline.
She called it *akeyí*, that's *den k'e*, Tagish language.
She made big sport day for them because she's going to leave them.
Falltime, she made it from bull moose skin.
There's no moose before that! Where she got that, I don't know!
Anyway, that's the story. It was bull moose skin.
She put it up right in the middle of Bennett Lake.
It had four strings.
One went to Grey Mountain, *Takaadí T'ooch'*. That means "Charcoal
        Mountain" in Tlingit.
One went to the mountain behind Chooutla school, *Métáatl'e
        Shéch'ée.*
That means "wind on the forehead" in Tagish language.
One went to Fourth of July Mountain: *Médzíh Dzéłe'* – that means
        "Caribou Mountain" –
and one went to that mountain we call *Chílíh Dzéłé'* – "Gopher
        Mountain."

They walked out on that line that ties the swing.
The first one to come is moose. Even that narrow, they walk on it!

Bull moose sings his song first:
"What is this they put out for me?
I'm walking on it, look at me."

They say he stepped through the skin he's so heavy.
Then the cow comes, then the calf. Each one has its song.
That calf can hardly stand up!

Then the caribou came with its young one –
by that time, they had young ones.
Then came sheep. All that were born, they sat on the swing.
Then wolf came and sang his song.
Then came the rabbit song. He says,
"My brothers always do that for me.
They chop down trees and give me food
and I always play around with it."

After she got through with that skin,
she told them she's going to part with them now.
"You go all into different countries.
Go!" she said.

Somebody was watching all this from way back there.
His name is *Tudech'ade.*

Animal Mother's Mountains. **1** Taaghahi (Tagish) "facing the water" / Ta̲kaadí T'ooch' (Tlingit) "charcoal rockslide"; **2** Métáatl'e Shéch'ée (Tagish) "wind blowing on the forehead" / Yaadéwduwanúk (Tlingit) "blowing against the face"; **3** Médzíh Dzéłe' (Tagish) "caribou mountain" / Watsíx Shaayí (Tlingit) "caribou mountain"; **4** Chílíh Dzéłe' (Tagish) "gopher mountain" / Tsálgi Shaayí (Tlingit) "gopher mountain". At the north end of Chílíh Dzéłe' is **5** Xóots Tláa Ta.eetí (Tlingit) "brown bear mother's sleeping place."

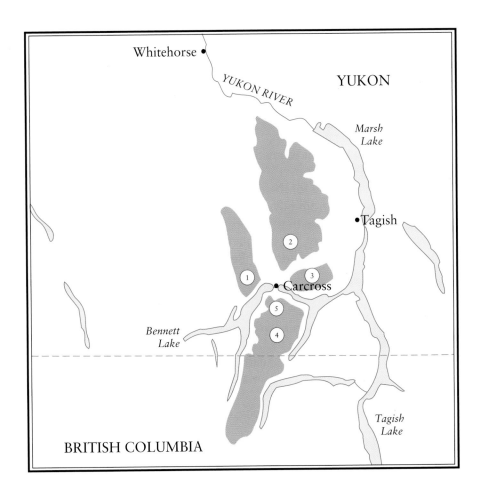

That means "duck head feathers" in Tagish language.
He saw when she parted with them.

She didn't go very far –
right to that *Chílíh Dzéłe'* at Carcross.
She camped there – that's where she slept.
They call it "grizzly bear mother's camp" – *Xóots Tláa Ta.eetí.*

Next day, she went to another mountain.
On top of the mountain, you see there's two big dips.
At the first camp she wasn't comfortable in that bed.
So she moved a little way from there to that Lanning Mountain –
    Kwákah Dzéłe'.

From there she went to Teslin – Three Aces, they call that mountain.
Right there they said there's a little bridge leads to a little mountain.
At that mountain they say there's a dip there, too.
Green grass grows around it.

From there, I don't know. . . .
That's as far as I remember.

Métáatl'e Shéch'ée, seen from across Nares Lake. The Tagish name for this mountain means "wind on the forehead." It now appears on maps as Caribou Mountain, while the mountain known as *Médzih Dzéłe'*, "Caribou Mountain" in the Tagish language, has acquired a different name in English. *Photo by Julie Cruikshank.*

Crow didn't want fish to come from saltwater this way, see? You see that Dezadeash Lake? It's about three miles [from Klukshu]. At Klukshu, they've got saltwater fish. But Crow made Dezadeash Lake come out the other side [draining north]. This side, different fish. He put his wing this way, that way [to establish the separate drainages].
– Mrs Annie Ned

Today there are four major drainage systems in the Yukon – two emptying into the Pacific Ocean and two into the Arctic.

The Yukon River is the dominant river crossing the Yukon Plateau, collecting runoff from about three quarters of the Territory. The Teslin, the Pelly, the Stewart, the White and the Porcupine, which are all major rivers in their own right, are tributaries of the Yukon. Water from these rivers crosses Alaska and empties into the Bering Sea – the northernmost extension of the Pacific.

The Alsek, which drains a part of the southwestern Yukon, cuts directly through the Coast Mountains, reaching the Pacific in the Gulf of Alaska instead of the Bering Sea.

The Peel, draining the north slope of the Ogilvie Mountains, and the Liard, draining the southeastern Yukon, form two additional watersheds, but both are tributaries of *Deh cho* (the Mackenzie River), which empties into the Beaufort Sea in the Arctic Ocean.

These river networks also connect many lakes. The large lakes of the southwestern Yukon, confined by mountains, lie near the boundary between the Yukon and Alsek watersheds, where drainage patterns are still affected by glacial action. Beach ridges, high above some of the present lake levels, suggest that much larger lakes were once trapped behind flanks of ice as the glaciers retreated thousands of years ago. The more numerous and smaller lakes of the northern Yukon, on the other hand, suggest the pattern of glacial scouring beneath the now vanished ice sheet.

Of all geological processes, running water must have the greatest impact on the lives of human beings. Rivers and lakes have been used for travel and fisheries throughout human history, and the patterns of flowing water have done much to determine where and how people could live throughout the world. But long before the present river systems of the Yukon existed, water in another form was moving more slowly over the earth and shaping the land where the rivers now flow.

A glacier forms when snow begins to pile up faster than it melts. Over time, the snow turns into ice. As ice thickens, its weight may cause it to flow, picking up soil and rock as it travels. Glaciers are capable of enormous erosion as they move through valleys, scraping the soil and exposing bedrock. The load of rock and debris carried by a glacier is eventually deposited, as the ice melts, and these deposits, called *moraines*, also have a role in shaping the physical landscape.

Between two and three million years ago, during the Pleistocene epoch, the earth experienced a major period of cooling. Since then, continental glaciers have repeatedly formed in the north, expanding to cover almost all of Canada and large parts of the United States. The most recent glaciation, the Wisconsin, retreated only 10,000 years ago, and remnants of these huge glaciers are found in the St Elias Mountains. Some parts of the Yukon were not glaciated during the last ice age, probably because the St Elias and Coast ranges blocked off moist Pacific air from the west and the Selwyn Mountains formed a barrier to the more easterly Laurentide ice sheet.

Glaciers in the St Elias Mountains are active remnants of the last ice age. Some are known as "surging glaciers" because periodically they begin to flow, sometimes for several kilometers and often quite rapidly. The Donjek Glacier, the Steele Glacier, the Lowell Glacier and many smaller glaciers have all surged in this century and will surge again. This is no surprise to elders who talk about similar surges during the last century.

The Lowell Glacier, for example, has crossed the Alsek River many times. In the 1940s, anthropologists Catharine McClellan and Frederica de Laguna heard elders tell how this glacier surged in 1852. In the 1980s, Mrs Kitty Smith was still telling the same story, as she had heard it from her own elders.

Mrs Smith calls the Lowell Glacier by its Southern Tutchone name, *Nàlùdi*, meaning "fish stop." The name *Nàlùdi* refers to a time in the past when the advance of this glacier stopped the migration of salmon to the upper Alsek drainage. She describes how Nàlùdi crossed the Alsek River to Goatherd Mountain where it grew to an enormous height. Scientists tell us that the ice built up to 200 m, damming an immense lake, Glacial Lake Alsek, that filled the Dezadeash and Alsek valleys right up to present-day Haines Junction.

Mrs Smith blames the surge on the arrogance of a young Yakutat Tlingit visitor to the Yukon who made fun of an Athapaskan shaman because of his balding head.

"Ah, that old man! The top of his head is just like the place gopher plays, a bare stump," said the visitor.

Another older Tlingit man warned him not to behave so rudely, but the damage was done. To punish him and his kinsmen, the shaman sat on the top of Goatherd Mountain and called the glacier across the Alsek River. A lake formed behind the flank of the glacier. Then the shaman broke the dam, causing a flood that scoured the landscape and drowned those Yakutat Tlingit camped at the junction of the Tatshenshini and Alsek rivers.

Nàlùdi has surged again several times, Mrs Smith says, most recently in her "grandmother's time," just before her own birth. One summer about 1890, some people travelled north to Kluane Lake while others stayed behind drying meat. Nàlùdi blocked the river, flooding the valley basin in just a few days and killing hundreds of ground squirrels before the dam burst and the lake drained.

Mrs Smith tells other stories about the surging of the Donjek Glacier in her book *Nindal Kwädindür*. Her explanations for the *causes* of surging differ from those offered by scientists. Scientists look for physical mechanisms. Oral tradition bearers more often look for moral relationships. Sometimes the narratives return us to a time long ago when giant animals competed with humans for control of the world; in these stories glaciers are the dens of giant animals and they surge when the animal is angered by thoughtless human behaviour. Together the two different approaches give us a richer sense of landscape than can be derived from either one alone.

Glaciers now cover about one tenth of the earth's surface. 18,000 years ago, they covered one third of the earth. Today, the volume of glacial ice on the earth is about 25,000,000 km^3. During the Ice Age it was closer to 70,000,000 km^3.

Many elders from the southwest Yukon know this story. Mrs Smith's version appears in her book *Nindal Kwädindür*, pp 87–88. See also Catharine McClellan's *My Old People Say*, pp 71–72, and Frederica de Laguna's *Under Mount St Elias*, p 276. There are also many stories about the Flood that occurred at the beginning of time; for a discussion of these, see Cruikshank, *When the World Began*, pp 9–10.

BERINGIA

CORDILLERAN ICE SHEET

LAURENTIDE ICE SHEET

North American glaciation in the last ice age.
Glacial geologists suggest that at times an
ice-free corridor may have opened between
the Laurentide and Cordillera ice sheets.

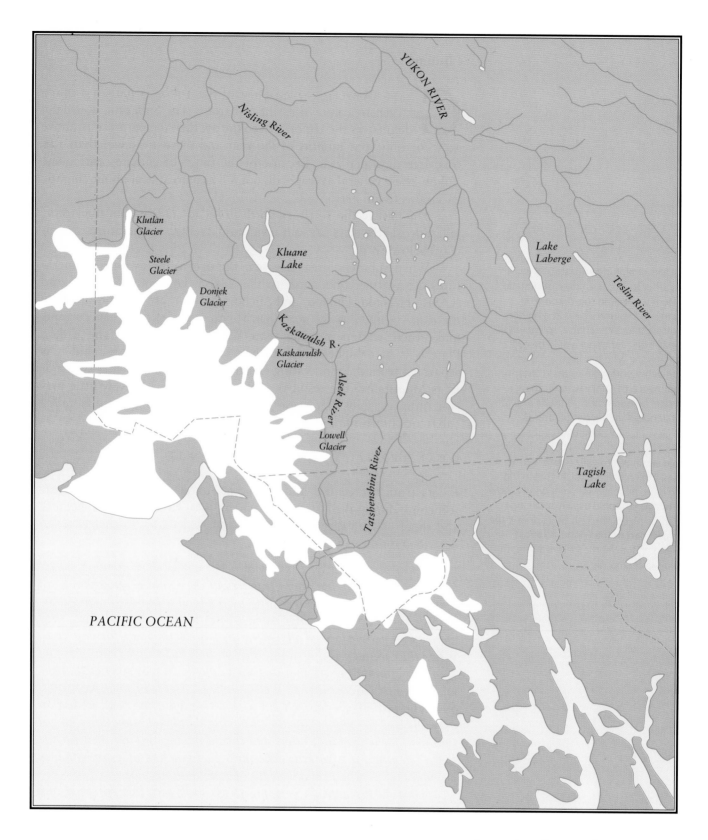

YUKON RIVER

Nisling River

Klutlan
Glacier

Steele
Glacier

Donjek
Glacier

Kluane
Lake

Kaskawulsh R.

Kaskawulsh
Glacier

Alsek River

Lowell
Glacier

Tatshenshini River

Lake
Laberge

Teslin River

Tagish
Lake

PACIFIC OCEAN

Present-Day Glaciers in the Yukon

Climate

GEOGRAPHICALLY, most of the Yukon is part of a much larger area known as the Subarctic. The Subarctic is usually defined as the region where the average temperature is above 10°C for only four months of the year and there are fewer than 120 frost-free days per year. Because of the range of climates within the Yukon, these general averages do not tell us a great deal about climatic variations found here.

The part of the Territory north of 66°32' falls within the *Arctic*, where frost-free days are still fewer and average temperatures are always below 10°C.

When subarctic areas are near the ocean, the average temperatures are warmer than those in the Yukon. For example, Leningrad (USSR), Helsinki (Finland) and Anchorage (USA) are at approximately the same latitude as the southern Yukon, but nearby ocean currents make their winters warmer than Whitehorse winters. The Yukon Plateau is at a higher altitude than coastal communities, and it is separated from the moderating ocean currents by the barrier of the St Elias Mountains. The result is a dry climate with relatively little precipitation annually. For these reasons, the Yukon's climate is called subarctic *continental*.

ORAL TRADITIONS ABOUT CLIMATE

Elders from the central and southern Yukon tell of a terrible year sometime during the last century when "two winters joined together" and there was no real summer. Tutchone elder Mrs Rachel Dawson described it this way in 1974:

I told you about that year summer never came? Two winters joined together. No snow, but there was ice all over, and the winters were joined together. Just about a little better than a hundred years now. Young moose born in springtime just froze to the ground. I guess they were wet – people looked all over in the woods, they say, for that kind. When they found a young moose frozen, they cut it up to eat. . . .

My grandfather's father dug up a lake . . . it was so cold that the lake was just frozen right to the bottom. Ice right through, no water. So my grandfather's father took a chisel – tandal they call it, Indian way. He dug the whole lake up – how big that lake! Sometimes he got two fish. He'd take that home and they'd make soup out of it for the kids. They had lots of kids, like me – I've got lots of grandchildren down there. . . . He'd eat a little bit of soup with his kids.

He told his wife, "I'm going to go look out, just to see if any moose are coming around."

He had no gun. They've just got bow and arrow.

He sat down under a tree. He got his packsack he sat on and rested. I guess he's tired and weak without eating. Starvation! A lot of people starved in the Yukon that time. He sat there and he heard something running . . . you could hear it run on the ice, ice breaking

Factors of altitude and latitude work together to create a range of climatic differences within the Yukon. For example, Dawson City is at a higher latitude than Whitehorse, so we might predict that summers would be cooler. But anyone who has lived in Dawson and Whitehorse knows that Dawson summers are usually warmer than Whitehorse summers. Altitude also influences summer temperatures.

In winter we sometimes get a situation called an *inversion*, when very cold air sinks into valleys and warmer air rises. Yukon elders explain that in the old days, people living near what is now Whitehorse would usually move up high, to places like Fish Lake, during the coldest part of the winter, to avoid spending time in the valleys during the mid-winter months.

under it. . . . So he opened his eyes and looked. He kept still. He got his bow and arrow ready . . . just held it. . . . Here that cow had come down to have her baby. He shot it. Just one shot and he got it. . . . He went home to tell his wife.

"We have to move," he said. "I can't pack all that meat. I've got a moose down there."

So they moved down and made camp right there. She cut the meat. She dried it. She cooked for the kids. Everything like that.

It is difficult to locate this year in chronological time, because oral traditions sometimes telescope events, or collapse the chronology. Many versions of this story have been recorded during the last forty years and no matter when the narrator tells it, it always seems to have occurred just about a hundred years earlier. One possibility is that it occurred around 1816, just after a major volcanic eruption of Tamboro, in Indonesia. Records from the eastern United States, England and Switzerland show that 1816 was the coldest year for which records exist. Scientists working with tree rings suggest that the years 1845, 1849, and 1850 were also exceptionally cold. The Hudson's Bay trader Robert Campbell reported extreme cold and scarcity in the central Yukon during those same years. Again, oral traditions may not actually make it easier to *date* events, but they deepen our understanding of what these events must have meant in peoples' lives.

Plants and Animals

WHAT LIVES on the land? The answers to this question depend to some extent on factors already discussed – geology, geography, water and climate. All of these factors affect soils, critical to growth of vegetation.

Yukon land is predominantly rock. While there are areas where soils have built up, permitting small-scale agriculture, Yukon soils are generally thin and support only limited vegetation.

Large areas of the Yukon soil are permafrost; that is, they are frozen throughout the year. Most of the Yukon is in an area of *discontinuous* permafrost, meaning that the soil thaws in some places and not in others. In the extreme northern Yukon, the ground is always frozen; in other words, the permafrost is *continuous*.

If we look at a map of vegetation in the Yukon, we find that, in a very general way, regions of vegetation parallel the geological divisions we discussed above. The extreme southwest is covered by glaciers and mountain outcrop and very little vegetation. Most of the southern Yukon supports *boreal forest*. This includes trees that can survive in thin soil which does not retain water – white spruce, black spruce, larch, subalpine fir, lodgepole pine, aspen, poplar, birch. Trees with deeper root systems need soil that retains water. Further north, as the zone of continuous permafrost begins to dominate, the trees get smaller and *shrubs* begin to take over. In the extreme north, trees disappear and *grasses* and *sedges* become the most common vegetation.

Climate is important in maintaining the boundary between boreal

Permafrost still affects major decisions we make about human activity in the North. During the Mackenzie Valley Pipeline Inquiry in 1975 and the Alaska Valley Pipeline Inquiry in 1976 a number of scientists expressed concerns about building pipelines across permafrost – both discontinuous (along the Alaska Highway) and continuous (along the Arctic coast).

The view from Goatherd Mountain.
Jack Schick is sitting at or near the spot
where the shaman made his decision to
call *Nàłùdi* across the Alsek River.
Photo by Julie Cruikshank.

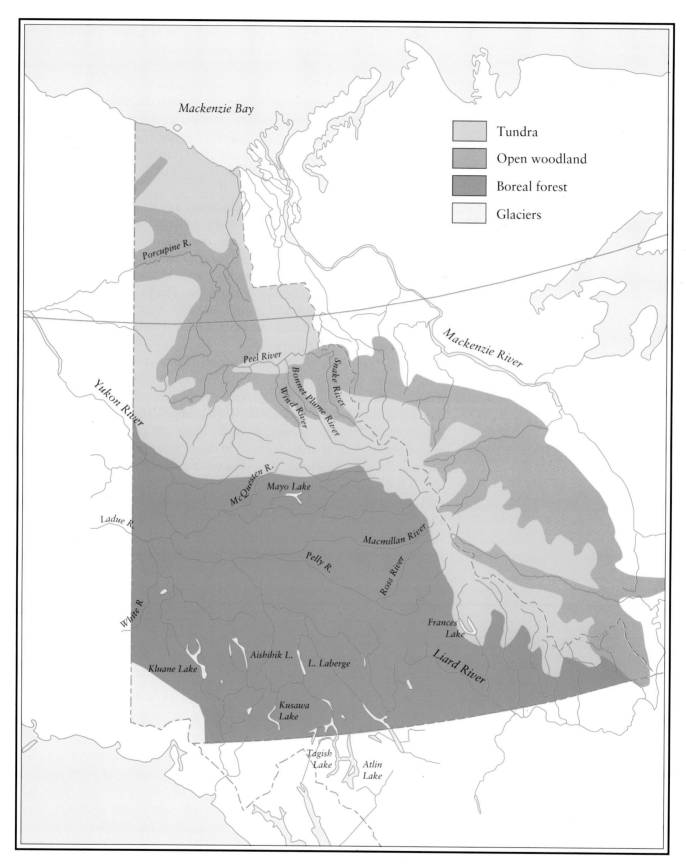

Mackenzie Bay

Porcupine R.

Yukon River

Peel River

Snake River

Bonnet Plume River

Wind River

Mackenzie River

McQuesten R.

Mayo Lake

Ladue R.

Macmillan River

Pelly R.

Ross River

White R.

Frances Lake

Aishihik L.

L. Laberge

Liard River

Kluane Lake

Kusawa Lake

Tagish Lake

Atlin Lake

Tundra

Open woodland

Boreal forest

Glaciers

Yukon vegetation

39

forest in the south and tundra in the north. The southwestern Yukon is influenced by moist Pacific air all summer, but the north is dominated by dry Arctic air all year. Some scientists think that global warming will cause the boreal forest to move much farther north.

We can see from a map of vegetation how *latitude* affects what grows on the land; when we look at a Yukon mountain we can also see how *altitude* affects plant growth as well. Forest cover is predominant in river valleys, on hills and lower mountain slopes. At higher altitudes, we see shrubs, berry bushes, low flowering plants, lichens, and rock. At some altitudes, snow cover remains all year.

All life depends on the productivity of land and water, and changes in Yukon ecology are generally reflected in changing animal populations. Thousands of years ago the Yukon had a different climate, with extensive grasslands and large grazing mammals. Not only were there animals we can see today – moose, caribou, sheep, bear, fox, beaver – there were also mastodons, elephants, woolly mammoths, giant beavers, ground sloths and sabre-toothed tigers. Archaeologists tell us that this was the landscape early humans found when they arrived in North America.

Oral traditions about animals and plants convey two kinds of information. On one hand there are fundamentally important narratives, the cornerstone of Athapaskan and Tlingit oral literature. These narratives address the balance between humans and the animals with whom they share the world. As well, there are precise observations about plants and animals passed on from generation to generation, often in the form of Tlingit and Athapaskan place names.

Oral traditions refer, for example, to shifting ranges of caribou and moose during the last century. Caribou used to range deep into the southern Yukon. In fact the name Carcross is shortened from its old name, Caribou Crossing. And the name *Médzíh É'oł*, "place where caribou swim across in groups," refers to a point on Nares Lake where caribou herds once crossed. Elders also refer to the presence of buffalo in the southeastern Yukon in the late 1900s. A character whose Tlingit name is *Xaas* (Wood Buffalo) turns up in some stories. And elders comment in fine detail on the varieties of fish in Yukon lakes, as well as changes that have occurred in fish populations. For example, the Tagish name *Dasgwáàge Méne'* (Squanga Lake) refers to a rare pygmy white fish puzzling to scientists because of its discontinuous distribution throughout North America.

Humans and Ecology

MANY important questions about past, present and future relationships among humans, animals and environment are being studied in the north. Because systematic scientific observations in the Yukon often date only to the 1930s or 1940s, the knowledge elders have about these changing relationships is particularly valuable.

During the last century, geographers and historians often speculated that climate and ecology cause human cultures to develop in

See *Part of the Land, Part of the Water* for a more detailed discussion of plants and animals living in the Yukon today.

specific ways. Initially, they tried to use examples from Arctic and Subarctic peoples to support their ideas. It now appears that there are no simple causal relationships like this. Environment certainly sets limits on the range of possibilities for human life, human history and human culture, but it does not *cause* any of these to develop in any particular way. In fact, the more we learn from Arctic and Subarctic cultures, the more we understand the wide variety of ways in which humans have learned to live and work in extreme environments.

Science and oral tradition present us with different, but equally valuable, ways of understanding relationships between environment, animals and humans. These ways of understanding can't easily be compared, because they have different objectives. Both traditions provide stimulating ideas as well as precise information. The issue is not which one is "better" but rather that knowing something about each may broaden our understanding of human history.

HOW ANIMALS BROKE THROUGH THE SKY

Angela Sidney

One time the sky used to come right down to salt water.
Here the animals lived on the winter side.
Cold.
Squirrel always came amongst other animals, crying all the time.

One time they asked her,
"What are you crying for?"

"My kids all froze up again."
Every now and then her children, her babies, all froze up.

So they went to a meeting, all the animals.
They are going to try to poke a hole through the sky.
They are on the winter side,
and they are going to poke a hole through the sky
so they can have summertime too.
Summer is on the other side.

So they gathered together with all kinds of people – they're animals,
    though.
Bloodsucker is the one they picked to go through that hole.
He poked that hole.
Then different animals went through.
Wolverine is the one who made that hole bigger.
He went through with a dry mooseskin,
made that hole bigger.
That's how they all got through.
Now they are going to steal good weather.

At the beginning of time, the horizon came down to the earth to make a barrier. On one side of the barrier was a snow-covered winter world, where everything was white – animals, people, and other living things. The other side was the world of ordinary reality, as we now understand it. In many of the oldest stories, people who are stolen away to the world of myth-time cross a barrier – going under a log or under a point of land that rises to give them passage – and arrive in this winter world. When the trader Robert Campbell first arrived in the Yukon in 1848, many people thought that he had come from this winter world because of his white skin. Angela Sidney tells how the first animals managed to cross to the summer world by having Bloodsucker, the Leech, make a hole in the barrier.

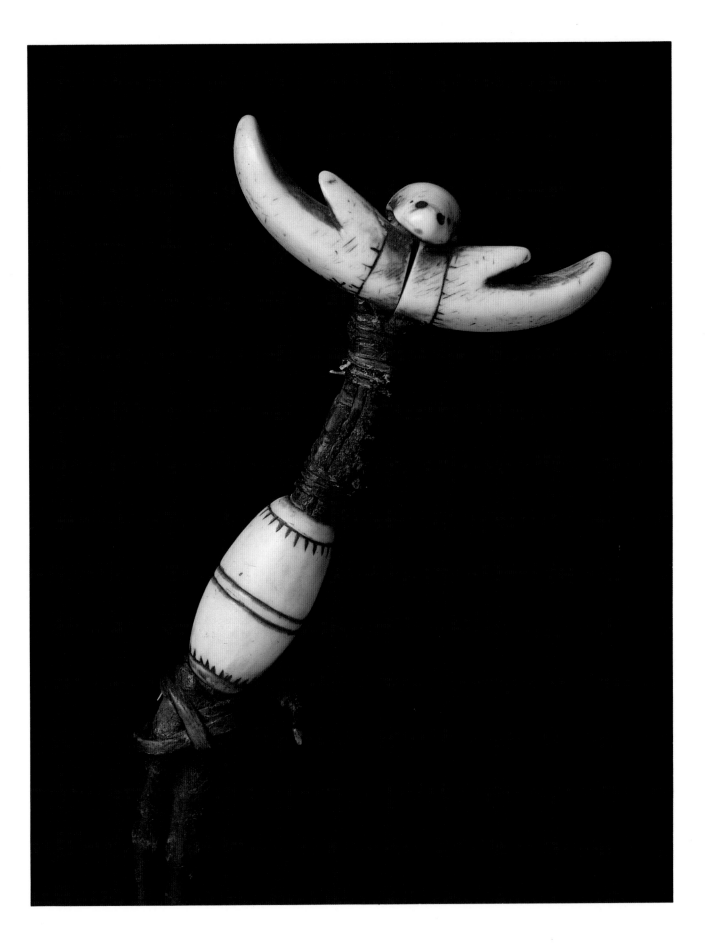

One end of an Inuvialuit snare from the
northern Yukon. The handle and toggle
are ivory. The photos are about twice
actual size. *McBride Museum,
Whitehorse. Yukon Government photo.*

3 Before Written Records

What happens when the
formalities . . . of "history" are
displaced into a dispersal of stories?
Who has stories to tell? What are
their methodologies? How do they
speak to their readers? What are the
tones of their voices?
– Barbara Kruger and Phil Mariani,
Remaking History, p ix

Where do these people come from?
Outside? You tell different stories
from us people. You people talk from
paper. Me, I want to talk from
Grandpa.
– Mrs Annie Ned, elder, speaking to
archaeologists at the Yukon Historical
and Museums Association meeting,
Haines Junction, Yukon, 1982

THE WRITING of history has always involved collecting, analyzing and retelling stories about the past. The very act of collection, though, means that some stories are enshrined in books and others left to shift for themselves. In Yukon history, stories passed by word of mouth are less likely to appear in books than those passed down in scientific papers and historical documents. Very often these accounts give smooth cause and effect explanations of "what really happened." But what about the missing voices?

This problem, of course, is not unique to the Yukon. Throughout the world, archaeologists and historians are becoming aware that accounts of the past often pay too much attention to Europeans and too little to the viewpoints of people who were living on the other five continents – North America, South America, Asia, Africa and Australia – when Europeans first arrived. Textbooks tell us that Christopher Columbus "discovered" America and the indigenous peoples living there. Native Americans respond, "We weren't discovered: we have always been here."

Lately, historians are making attempts to include accounts of First Peoples' history when they write about the past. But rewriting history is a complicated business; it can't be done by adding an introductory chapter to an existing history book. In Canada, for example, First Nations rightly point out that sandwiching a chapter on aboriginal peoples between a chapter on "geography and environment" and a chapter on "the fur trade" gives another mixed message. It suggests that First Nations existed in the past but do not live on in the present. It traps them in history or even *prehistory*.

The term prehistory seems to suggest a time before history began. Dictionaries usually define prehistory as a time before written records. But for people who have always relied on the spoken word to pass on information, this dictionary definition is not very meaningful. For Canada's First Nations, these earlier periods *are* their history, and they reject the term prehistory altogether.

Investigations of the earliest periods of Yukon history have focussed on two questions. The first – how and when did aboriginal peoples come to this part of North America? – is the subject of this chapter. The second question – how were aboriginal peoples living at the time when the first Europeans arrived? – is discussed in Chapter 4.

Origins of Yukon Peoples: Oral Traditions

ELDERS and archaeologists give different versions of how humans came to be living in the area now called the Yukon. This is because they begin with different questions.

When Yukon elders talk about human origins, they are less concerned about *where* people came from than with *how* people became fully human. In these accounts, the order in which events occurred is not always entirely clear or even very important, and the key figures differ in different parts of the Yukon. In the southern Yukon, for example, Crow created people, but he created them in a world where animals already existed. Animal Mother brought animals into the world quite independently of Crow, but at their birth she reminded them that they were "born from people" and should not make trouble for them. At the beginning of time, animals and humans could communicate directly with one another, but were not entirely suited to living in the world together. Because humans and animals had to share the world, their first task was to learn how to get along together and how to respect each other's power.

Taken together, narratives explore different aspects of a comprehensive world view. Some narratives tell how Beaverman taught *animals* the correct ways to behave toward people. Others dramatize the ways the Two Smart Brothers had to teach *people* how to behave so that they could survive in the world. Still other stories show what happens when humans forget that they are only one of many species and display human arrogance. In these stories, a person who mistreats or offends an animal species is taken on a journey to relearn the knowledge given to humans at the beginning of time.

As well as learning how to share power with other animals, humans had to learn how to live with each other. At the same time that Crow made people, he set in motion a social order which still is very important today. (We discuss this in detail in Chapter 4.) He divided people into two groups, Wolf and Crow. Each child automatically belongs to the same kinship group as his or her mother and is expected to marry someone from the opposite group.

Even though the chronology or sequence may not be important in the stories of Crow, Beaverman (or *Äsùya*), the Two Smart Brothers, and Animal Mother, *place* usually is important. One thing elders agree about is that creatures native to the Yukon were created here, and that the Yukon has always been their home. Narratives told by Yukon elders convey a sense that time and space have some unity and are not easily separated. This picture contrasts with the one presented by western science and history, where physical places are assumed to be distinct and separate, and where time is understood to follow a linear progression.

Archaeology is a specialized branch of anthropology. Archaeologists study physical, material remains, usually from the past. They interpret the direct and indirect record of human activity preserved in those remains.

See, for example, the stories of "The Boy Who Stayed with Fish" and "The Man Who Stayed with Groundhog Woman" told by Mrs Kitty Smith and Mrs Angela Sidney in *My Stories Are My Wealth*, pp 45–57.

CROW

Angela Sidney

Then Crow disappears.
He has those things with him in a box.
He walks around – comes to a river.
Lots of animals there – fox, wolf, wolverine, mink, rabbit.
Everybody's fishing. . . .
That time animals all talk like people talk now –
the world is dark.

"Give me fish," Crow says.
No one pays attention.
"Give me fish or I'll bring daylight!"
They laugh at him.

He's holding a box . . . starts to open it and lets one ray out.
Then they pay attention!
He opens that box a bit more – they're scared!
Finally he opens that daylight box and threw it out.
Those animals scatter!
They hide in the bush and turn into animals like now.
Then the sun, moon, stars and daylight come out.

"Go to the skies," Crow says.
"Now no one man owns it – it will be for everybody."

He's right, what he says, that Crow.

Stories of Crow's role in creation are told throughout much of northwestern North America – on the Pacific Northwest Coast (where he is called the Raven), in British Columbia, in the Yukon Territory, and even in northeast Asia. In southern Yukon traditions like the story Mrs Kitty Smith tells on pp 14–17, Crow brings light, fire and fresh water to the world. Many elders tell how he stole daylight by transforming himself into a pine needle. A woman swallowed him in that form, then gave birth to him as a human baby. Her father – now the reborn Crow's new grandfather – owned the sun, moon and stars, which he hoarded in his house.

After he was born, Crow tricked his grandfather into letting him play with these treasures – first with the sun and then with the moon and stars. The unsuspecting tyrant allowed his grandchild to roll them around on the floor. But once he had them all in his possession, Crow rolled them out the door and disappeared himself!

For a fuller version of this narrative, see Angela Sidney's *My Stories Are My Wealth*, pp 1–21.

Mrs Angla Sidney always begins her life story with reference to her Deisheetaan Crow clan. Born in 1902, near Carcross, her parents were *Ła.oos Tláa* (Maria) and *Kaajinéek'* (Tagish John). She was the eldest daughter in her family and learned a great deal about her Tagish and Tlingit ancestry, languages and traditions from her mother. She raised a large family and has been actively involved in community work in Carcross during her entire adult life. She began working with anthropologist Catharine (Kitty) McClellan in 1947 and has continued that work with other anthropologists, with linguists and with children since that time. She has narrated several books of oral narratives and life history and was awarded the Order of Canada in 1986. Mrs Sidney is the last fluent speaker of the Tagish language.

Postscript: Angela Sidney died in Whitehorse on 17 July 1991, while the printing of this book was underway.

Angela Sidney

Longer versions of the Game Mother or Animal Mother story by Mrs Kitty Smith and Mrs Angela Sidney appear in *My Stories Are My Wealth,* pp 85–92. In this excerpt, Mrs Sidney tells how Animal Mother gave birth to all the animals and advised them of their responsibilities to people.

Here she started to grow, bigger and bigger and bigger like that.
And she wouldn't go anyplace, wouldn't travel around.
She was just so big.

Springtime, that's the time when animals are born.
She told her husbands,
"It's no use [waiting] because I'm no good to you people.
You'd better go on your own.
Just leave me right here.
But make a better housecamp for me."
That's what she told them.
"If you want to, you can watch me from a long ways away,
from on top of the mountain."

Anyway, they left.
They hated to go, but they had to go anyway.
They watched, I guess, all the time.
I wonder what kind of fieldglasses they got, eh?

The first thing they know, moose was born.
As soon as those husbands go, those animals came out!
Moose had grizzly teeth too, they say.
She called it back and she took those teeth out.

Origins of Yukon Peoples: Archaeology

ARCHAEOLOGISTS ask different *questions* about human origins from those asked by elders. That is one of the reasons why they often come up with different answers. One major problem that interests archaeologists is when and how people first came to be living in the Western Hemisphere or North America. Consequently, they are more concerned than elders about ordering events in a sequence, or establishing absolute dates. They are particularly interested in Yukon research because most of them believe that the ancestors of all Native American people once passed through the Yukon.

They look for two kinds of evidence: physical remains (typically human and animal bones), and what they refer to as material culture – objects either deliberately or accidentally modified by humans. New stories are continually emerging from this material culture: stories about the ten-thousand-year period between the end of the last ice age and the nineteenth century when the first Europeans arrived.

On a world scale, archaeological evidence suggests that humans originated in the warm, low-latitude forests of Africa. As human populations spread out, they had to learn new strategies for survival, partic-

She showed moose what to eat – willow.
Bull moose came with a horn.
"Leave your horn once in a while," she told him.
"Don't use it all of the time, just in running season."
Then she told moose to lick salt in her ashes.
That's why they lick mud all the time, looking for salt.
They call it moose lick.

Caribou came next – first bull and then cow.
Bull caribou came with horns too, so she told him the same thing.
"Leave your horns once in a while.
Don't use them all the time, just in running season.
Just then you use it," she told them.
And she taught them to eat moss.

Next sheep came, and she taught him to eat grass.

Then came grizzly – she tried to call him back to take his teeth out,
      but he wouldn't come.
She couldn't get it!

"I'm going to use these teeth to get even," he told her.
"You're taking everything from us."

"Well, don't be mean to people," she told him.
"Remember that you came from people."

---

ularly as they moved north and encountered unfamiliar climates. Winters are extremely cold in the Subarctic, so before people could live in northern regions, they had to master the use of fire. They also had to develop techniques for making tailored skin clothing and warm, secure shelters. There were fewer species of plants and animals than at lower latitudes, and they were available only at certain times of the year, so people had to invent specialized hunting, fishing and gathering techniques as well as methods for storing food. They probably developed specialized watercraft for travelling on large bodies of cold water. In the scientific study of human cultural development, archaeological evidence from the Arctic and Subarctic is very important because it provides a record of the range of new skills people had to learn before they could pass *through* these environments to reach North America.

The most recent major glaciation, known as the Wisconsin, lasted from 30,000 to 10,000 years ago and covered most of Canada. Not all of northern North America was ice-covered, however. As Arctic waters became locked into ice, the shallow bed of the Bering Sea was exposed, joining northwestern Asia, Alaska and the northern Yukon in a large subcontinent called *Beringia*. Often described as a "land bridge" joining the Old and New Worlds, Beringia was actually a substantial land mass stretching 1500 km from north to south.

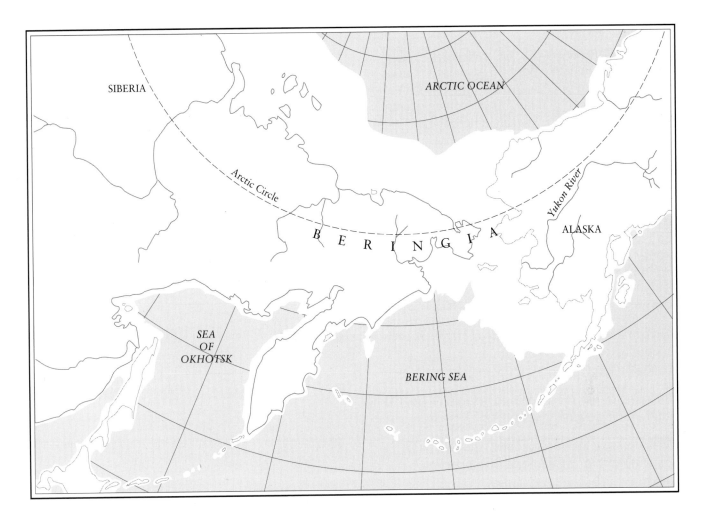

Beringia: the Asia-North America connection. The white area represents land above sea level during the last glaciation.

Biologists call vegetation in early Beringia *steppe tundra,* and say that this ecosystem is now extinct: there is no modern equivalent. More productive than modern tundra, it has been compared to the rich and tropical savannah grasslands of Africa.

If animals inhabited Beringia, people probably did as well. Archaeologists say that it is likely that people were living in western Beringia (northeast Asia) 35,000 years ago. But with the melting of the glaciers 10,000 years ago, the seas rose again, eliminating entire plant communities and possibly driving out the animals and humans who relied on them. Archaeologists studying Beringia now are restricted to working in unglaciated parts of Asia, Alaska and the Yukon, because elsewhere all evidence has been scoured away by the Wisconsin glaciation or submerged by rising seas.

A related question, of course, is when people might have travelled south of the glacial barrier to reach continental North America. During most of Beringia's existence, the Laurentide and Cordillera glaciers met, forming a barrier that was essentially impassable, though some archaeologists think that it may have been open at times. Archaeologists disagree about whether people actually managed to travel across Beringia and south of that barrier during the Wisconsin glaciation.

Beaverman is a hero who was active during a time when the distinction between animals and humans was less rigid than it is now. He has different names in different parts of the Yukon. Kaska speakers call him *Tsuquya*. Southern Tutchone speakers call him *Äsùya;* his Tlingit name is *Geidiyedi;* in Tagish stories he appears as *Cha'kwaza.*

Beaverman is human, but he can change into a beaver when the situation requires, and he uses this to his advantage when he finds himself in difficulty. He leaves his familiar surroundings and goes off to kill a series of monsters – giant men and animals – that are terrorizing people on the Yukon River. He undergoes dangerous ordeals, uses his powers to reduce giant animals to their present size, and ultimately makes the Yukon River safe for human beings.

If Beaverman makes the world safe for humans, the Two Brothers teach humans how to live responsibly in the world. They also travel down a river (which Mrs Sidney identifies as the Mackenzie River in her narrative). They meet people who are new to the world and are trying to understand how to live. They teach them what to eat and how to eat it. They even instruct them about the proper way to give birth. They encounter giants in their travels who are dangerous but dull-witted and easily outsmarted. Finally, they manage to complete their journey and to return home safely.

See *My Stories Are My Wealth,* pp 22–38 and 39–44 for versions of these stories.

Most archaeologists believe that people arrived south of the glacial barrier sometime between 15,000 and 12,000 years ago.

Archaeologists are also interested in establishing cultural sequences in the Yukon *following* the last glaciation. One of the best documented of these cultural sequences is in the southwest part of the Territory. Briefly, the oldest known archaeological site in the southwest Yukon is at Canyon Creek, where the Alaska Highway crosses the Aishihik River. It represents a 7200-year-old camp, and archaeologists believe that it overlooked grasslands that developed when the immense Glacial Lake Champagne drained about nine thousand years ago. You can climb up to this height of land from the Alaska Highway, look south over the forest and imagine how it must have looked thousands of years ago when this was a cool grassland country inhabited by bison.

The next several thousand years saw continuing changes in climatic conditions and corresponding cultural adaptations. The early postglacial period must have been characterized by a cold dry climate with periodic flooding while lakes established their drainages. Not all of these drainages were stable; for example, Kluane Lake originally drained south to the Pacific Ocean via the Slims River; it cut its present drainage north to the Yukon River only 300 to 400 years ago.

The changing drainages of Kluane Lake.
When the flow southward was
interrupted by the advance of the
Kaskawulsh Glacier, the lake level rose
until a new outlet to the north was
created.

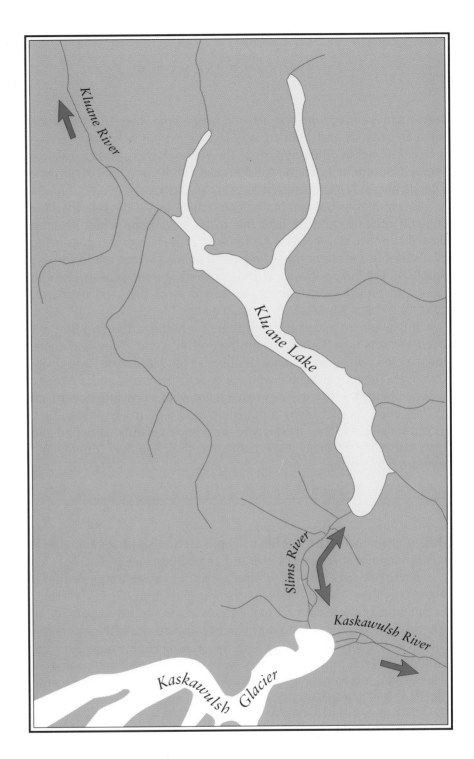

Khane River

Khane Lake

Slims River

Kaskawulsh River

Kaskawulsh Glacier

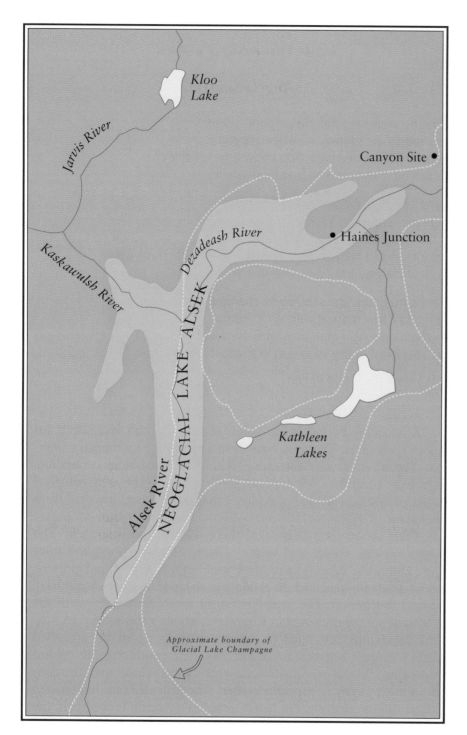

Kloo Lake

Jarvis River

Kaskawulsh River

Dezadeash River

Canyon Site •

• Haines Junction

NEOGLACIAL LAKE ALSEK

Alsek River

Kathleen Lakes

Approximate boundary of
Glacial Lake Champagne

Approximate extent of Neoglacial Lake Alsek. Glacial Lake Champagne probably disappeared about 9000 years ago, in the long, slow process of warming that followed the Wisconsin glaciation. The considerably smaller Neoglacial Lake Alsek formed and drained in the same region several times. The most recent of these neoglacial lakes, shown here, drained about 1850.

HOW THE WORLD BEGAN

Angela Sidney

From *My Stories Are My Wealth*, p 3.

After, he walks around, flies around alone.
He's tired – he's lonely – he needs people.
He took poplar tree bark. You know how it's thick?
He carved it and then he breathed into it.

"Live," he said. And he made a person.
He made Crow and Wolf too.
At first they can't talk to each other –
Crow man and woman are shy with each other – look away.
Wolf, same way too.

"This is no good," he said. So he changed that.
He made Crow man sit with Wolf woman
And he made Wolf man sit with Crow woman.
So Crow must marry Wolf and Wolf must marry Crow.

That's how the world began.

A warming period began some 6000 years ago and lasted for almost 3000 years. This must have been a good time for human habitation. The glaciers were retreating. The grasslands were expanding. Bison were plentiful. New types of tools appear in the archaeological record, providing one kind of evidence that people were attracted from other areas.

Then about 3000 years ago, there was an abrupt change. The climate became cooler and wetter. Glaciers began to expand once again. Lakes like Glacial Lake Alsek were impounded behind glaciers. Forests gradually replaced the eroding grasslands. Bison may not have survived this period. The final blow must surely have come with the volcanic eruption discussed in Chapter 2, about 1200 years ago. Climatic conditions continued to deteriorate right up to the so-called "Little Ice Age" between 1700 and 1850 AD, producing the coldest temperatures in the previous 10,000 year period. These were the conditions met by early European travellers who provided our first written descriptions of northwestern North America – Martin Frobisher in the late 1500s, Henry Hudson in 1610, Samuel Hearne in 1770, Alexander Mackenzie in 1789, John Franklin in 1820 and Robert Campbell in 1848. The journals they left behind describe conditions considerably more extreme than those experienced in the twentieth century, but their accounts have continued to influence perceptions of Arctic and Subarctic climates.

The people who successfully adapted to these changing conditions were the ancestors of the men, women and children whom Europeans met when they first came to this area. We often hear the word

Date	General Sequence	Cultural Sequence
150–100 BP	Lake Alsek	Bennett Lake
300–150 BP	Little Ice Age (1680 – 1820 AD)	Aishihik
350–130 BP	Kluane Lake drainage shifts	
1200 BP	White River Volcano	
2600 BP	Onset of Neoglaciation	Taye Lake
3300 BP	Abrupt transition from warm dry to cool wet climate	
	Dry grasslands	
	Soil deposited (8,000 – 3,000 BP)	Little Arm
6000 BP	Onset of warmer period	
7200 BP	Earliest archaeological site in southwest Yukon found so far	
9000 BP	Probable draining of Lake Champagne	
12,500 BP	Wisconsin glacier retreats near Kluane Lake	

This sequence begins with the most recent events and works back to the retreat of the last glaciation. Dates followed by BP refer to dates "Before Present"; actually all these dates work from a baseline of 1950 AD.

"traditional" – implying stable and unchanging – used to describe the cultures of aboriginal people who met the first Europeans. But only cultures willing and able to remain flexible and innovative in their responses to deteriorating environmental conditions could have survived such changes. People must always have been making adaptations to shifting habitations of plants, animals and fish. Part of the task of reconstructing the past is to determine how people made the choices they did. As we move closer to the recent period, archaeologists, like anthropologists and linguists, are working directly with elders, attempting to combine material culture, written records and spoken traditions to reconstruct that picture.

For a more detailed discussion of this cultural sequence, see *Part of the Land, Part of the Water*, Chapter 3.

The Archaeological Sequence

THE NAMES given by archaeologists to Yukon cultural sequences are sometimes confusing, because they identify *time periods* but refer to specific *geographical locations* where the materials representing this culture were first found.

The term *Little Arm* is used to refer to a widespread culture that existed from the end of the Wisconsin glaciation until 4500 years ago, but the name comes from a site where the tools were first excavated,

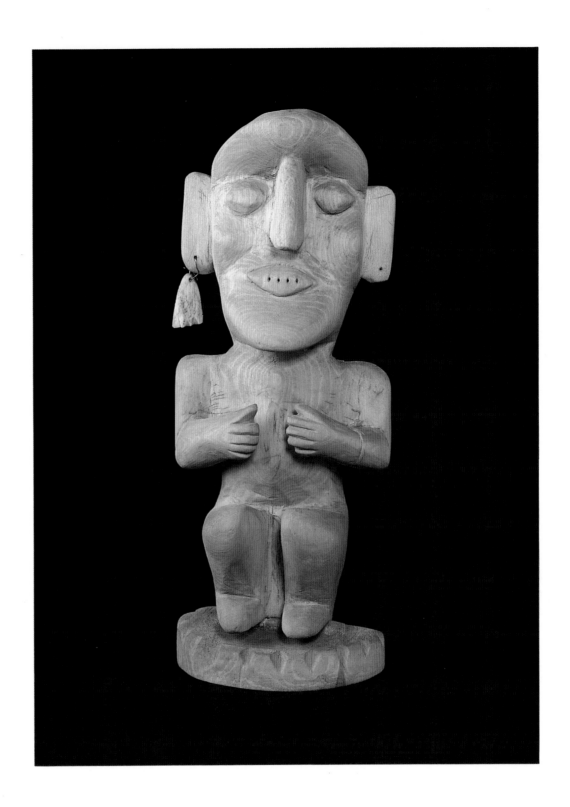

on Kluane Lake. The characteristic *Little Arm* tools are tiny razor-sharp microblades that could be mounted on a handle for very precise tasks. There were many other kinds of tools too, of course, but these are the most distinctive and are widespread during the entire period.

Archaeologists believe that about 4500 years ago, new people moved in from somewhere else, possibly from the northwest, completely replacing the Little Arm culture (except in the central Yukon where the Little Arm culture seems to have continued for another 2000 years). The new culture is named *Taye Lake*, again after a lake-side site on the Mendenhall River system. Taye Lake people were adapting to a colder, wetter, deteriorating climate where glaciers were expanding and conditions were decidedly uncomfortable. Their tools look quite different from microblades, with a characteristic notched point.

As if people were not already under enough pressure, the eruption of the White River Volcano 1200 years ago covered much of the southern Yukon with a layer of ash. This ash is a clear marker between Taye Lake culture and the next sequence, which is called *Aishihik* culture. The two are actually very similar except that the Aishihik culture has the addition of bows, arrows and copper arrowheads. The ash layer makes it very easy for archaeologists to see the transition.

A more recent cultural sequence, called *Bennett Lake*, covers the much shorter period between 1800 and 1900 AD. It is marked by the appearance of trade goods, indicating involvement in the European fur trade.

Archaeological research remains in early stages in the Yukon and has been possible only in scattered pockets. The earliest record of people – some 12,000 to 17,000 years ago – occurs at the Bluefish Caves site near Old Crow. An Inuit site on the Arctic coast (known as the Engigstciak site) is about 3500 years old. A site on the Porcupine River, called Klo-kut, shows over 1000 years of continuous occupancy as a caribou hunting village.

In their current work at Fort Selkirk, Peel River and Kusawa Lake, some archaeologists are working closely with elders to combine their different kinds of knowledge about life during the nineteenth century.

The carving on the facing page was made many years ago by Mrs Kitty Smith. Her father, Tàkàtà, was known for his work in wood and silver. Mrs Smith herself started carving after her marriage, when she and her husband were living near the Wheaton River.

This carving, which is 33 cm high, is made from poplar, and Mrs Smith calls it *Àjanà Zhaya*, "Got Lost." When she talks about the carving, she tells Crow stories – particularly stories in which Crow makes elaborate promises and then disappears. One of the stories begins like this:

That big tree, poplar tree, rotten inside. Crow cleans him inside. He clean him. "I'm going to fix some of you people yet."

"Ah," they say. "Always he talks too smart, that man."

Gone. He got lost!

The carving itself also got lost for many years, but it is now in the McBride Museum, Whitehorse. *Yukon Government photo.*

A couple on the Yukon River, about 1900. *Yukon Archives.*

Comparing Oral and Written Records: The Nineteenth Century 4

THERE ARE TWO kinds of remembered history from the late nineteenth-century Yukon, one oral and one written. These memories differ because the tellers had different goals and objectives. Consequently, they had different understandings of events. Written records from the Yukon do not date back so very many years — a few fur trade journals from the 1850s, travellers' reports from the 1880s and 1890s, a flood of letters and diaries from visitors who recorded *their own* stories during the Klondike gold rush. The histories constructed from these written accounts contain the visions of people who considered themselves "explorers" writing about their impressions of a land they thought they were discovering. In contrast, oral histories transmitted through narratives, songs, place names and genealogies reflect an understanding of the land and events from people who have always considered the Yukon their home.

Even though both oral and written accounts refer to the *past*, they are usually told in order to make a statement about the *present*. In other words, their purpose is to provide some background for explaining events that are happening *now*. They do this by emphasizing some events and by leaving out others. Both oral and written accounts about the past are *interpretations* which may change as circumstances change. The topics we consider in this chapter refer to the past, but they also reflect issues that concern people now: language, land use, material culture, and social life. At another time in history, or in another setting, other topics might be more important.

When Yukon Natives began doing research for land claims in the 1960s, one of their initial objectives was to document their common, *shared experiences* as the Yukon's First Nations. With the settlement of the claim, they are developing ways of working together while respecting longstanding regional and *cultural differences* within the Yukon. They point out that they chose carefully when they selected the term "First Nations" to refer to themselves, because they *are* more than one nation and speak with more than one voice. This chapter explores some of the cultural differences in the Yukon during the 1800s through the voices of elders from a few communities. Readers may discover that language, land use, material culture and social life are discussed differently by elders in other communities.

Anthropologists have attempted to reconstruct a picture of nineteenth-century cultural history in the Yukon. Anthropology is the

History is the shaping of the past by those living in the present. All histories derive from a particular time, a particular place, and a particular cultural heritage.
– Judith Binney, *New Zealand Journal of History*, 21(1), p 16.

I tell only what I know. Who[ever] tells you another story, ask him.
– Mrs Annie Ned, 1984

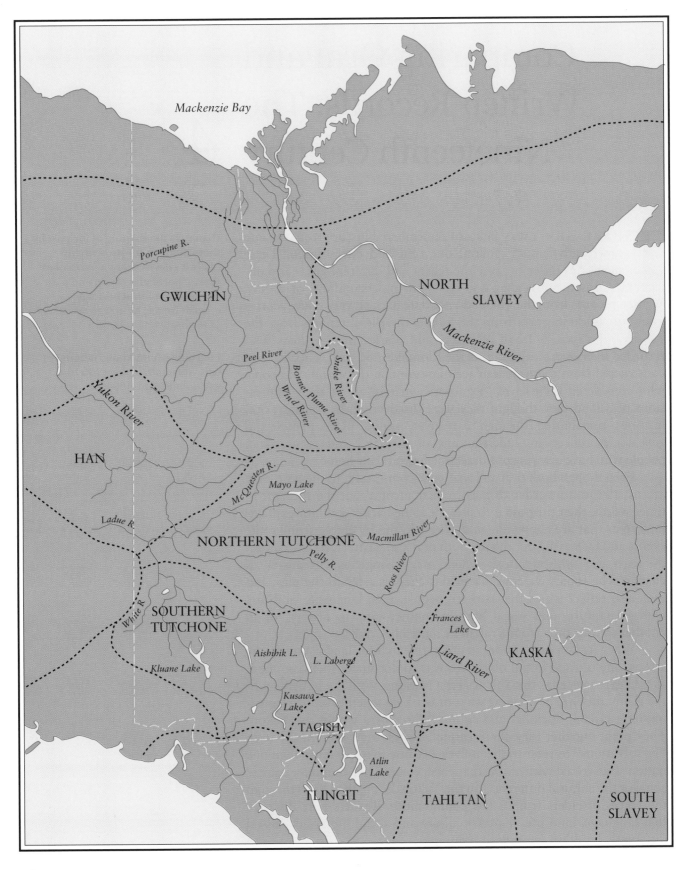

Yukon Native Languages

comparative study of human cultures. The accounts anthropologists write do not give the same picture a cultural "insider" would give, but they do provide a comparative framework for talking about similarities and differences between cultures.

Yukon Languages

MAPS of the Yukon showing territorial boundaries usually have lines separating different *language* groups. It is important to know several things about these maps.

First, linguistic maps like the one shown here refer to *language* groups, not to separate *territorial* or *political* groups. To some extent, language boundaries coincide with river drainages: the Peel, the Liard, and the Alsek are good examples. But boundaries between language groups are only approximate. The lines are never as firm or as clear as they appear on maps. Furthermore, no map made at the present time can be completely accurate for earlier periods. For example, people from the Taye Lake, Aishihik and Bennett Lake cultures described in Chapter 3 probably spoke Athapaskan languages, but we do not know how similar their languages were to Southern Tutchone, the language now spoken in the southwestern Yukon. Nor do we know how many other Athapaskan languages once spoken in the Yukon might have disappeared.

Second, it is important to remember that these are distinct languages, not dialects. They are as different from each other as, for example, English, French, Spanish and Italian. For a long time, many outsiders had the incorrect idea that all Yukon First Nations spoke one language. This led to serious communication problems as well as to errors on maps. A map of Native Peoples of Canada, widely circulated for many years by the branch of the Federal Government responsible for administering "Indian Affairs" gave one term – "Kutchin" – for the Yukon, as though all Native peoples in the Territory spoke one language. The word "Kutchin" is an attempt to write the name of the language spoken in Old Crow (now written *Gwich'in*). The language spoken in the central Yukon is Tutchone. In the Tutchone language, "Kutchin" sounds like an entirely different word. Tutchone-speaking elder Mrs Rachel Dawson used to point out that in *her* language "Kutchin" sounds a bit like *k'och'èn*, meaning "cloud people" – the word Tutchone speakers use for "white man." She used to comment wryly, "White men come here and take our land. Isn't that enough? Then they use our language to write 'white man' on the Yukon map!"

A third point to remember when studying the map of Yukon languages is that, even though linguistic terms are used more carefully now, they are still terms devised by outsiders. The earliest visitors wrote these names down more than a century ago, by asking people where they were from and writing down what they heard. When asked this question now, Mrs Annie Ned has patiently and repeatedly explained that this is not a very useful question. "People used to walk around all the time," she replies. Nor do elders consider their place of birth a particularly meaningful way to refer to themselves. Asked

Culture is a basic concept in anthropology. One problem with the term *culture* is that people use it to mean different things. In everyday conversation, people from western societies may use it to refer to art, dance or theatre.

We have seen that archaeologists refer to distinctive kinds of artifacts as representing cultures. Anthropologists use the term to mean something quite specific. They are referring to culture as a set of ideas or beliefs shared by members of a society that guide how those people behave. First Nations are developing their own definitions of how the term *culture* expresses their past and present ways of life.

All of these perspectives are combined in Catharine McClellan's *Part of the Land, Part of the Water*. The following pages direct the reader to specific sections in that book for further reading.

Yukon languages belong to two distinct *language families:* Tlingit and Athapaskan. Tlingit is spoken both in southeastern Alaska and in the southern Yukon. Athapaskan languages include at least thirty distinct languages spoken in the Yukon, Alaska, Northwest Territories, northern British Columbia, and northern Alberta as well as several spoken far to the south, including Navajo and Apache. Yukon Athapaskan languages are Loucheux (or Gwich'in), Han, Tutchone, Southern Tutchone, Tagish and Kaska. For a discussion of the history of the Yukon languages, see *Part of the Land, Part of the Water*, Chapter 6. An excellent overview of contemporary Yukon Native languages and issues associated with language maintenance, including personal statements about the ongoing importance of these languages, appears in *Speaking Out*, by Southern Tutchone linguist Daniel Tlen.

Daniel Tlen

This is an excerpt from Daniel Tlen's report *Speaking Out,* prepared in 1986 for the Yukon Government and the Council for Yukon Indians.

Yukon native languages must become more *visible.* They must have a higher, "up-front" profile than is presently the case. Signs must be erected in the native communities and along Yukon highways to identify local place names and sites of historical or mythological significance. Advertisements in the newspapers must begin to feature Yukon languages. The native language content in radio broadcasts must be increased. *Native languages should be seen and heard wherever a community of native speakers exists.* This will demonstrate that native people respect their own culture.

Yukon native languages must continue to grow, that is, to evolve from a highly developed oral system to a highly technical literate system. Literacy has begun to play a role in teaching programs and in community workshops. The growth and expansion of curriculum to include high school and university courses is also a necessity.

There is much hope for the future of Yukon native languages. That future will be defined mostly by the native people themselves, who must speak out about language and all the other things they believe important to them and their children.

---

where he was born, Johnny Johns always used to smile and say, "I was born under a tree." People travelled in the nineteenth century even more than they do now, so speakers of any one language might move, marry or travel to other parts of what is now the Yukon.

Elderly speakers of Yukon languages use other terms to refer to themselves. Most Yukon speakers of Athapaskan languages might begin by calling themselves *dän* or *den,* meaning "the people." Elders don't usually speak of themselves as belonging to a group with fixed boundaries. They are more likely to identify with groups of related people than with territorial groups. They might, for instance, describe themselves as either Crow (*kajìt*) or Wolf (*agunda*). If they were from the southern Yukon they might also make reference to their clan – *Deisheetaan, Dakl'aweidí, Yanyeidí, Gaanaxteidí* or one of the other clans prominent among inland Tlingit people.

Because there are so many different ways to say who you are, Yukon First Nations are now using *language* names to distinguish regional differences. The expansion of Native language programs in the Yukon during the 1980s indicates the significance language continues to have.

Land Use

UNDERSTANDING past and present land use in the Yukon has been particularly important for Yukon First Nations in recent years during ongoing negotiations of their land claims with the federal government. When elders talk about where they used to live, they usually describe their lives in terms of travel. Their understanding of land ownership is unlikely to include formal boundaries. Different headmen might claim ownership of certain land areas on behalf of their extended kinship group, but they would not refuse access to visitors. In the nineteenth century, families travelled very large distances each year, so members of any group might travel to several other parts of the country.

By the middle of the last century, people living in the Yukon were hunters and fishers who had made long-term and successful adaptations to a Subarctic environment. They depended on resources that varied from place to place and from season to season. These resources provided them with food, clothing and shelter, but they had to be prepared to move and to adjust the size of their group as the seasons and resources required. In the spring, muskrats, beaver and other fur-bearing animals were plentiful. In summers the salmon streams were teeming with fish. In the fall, people might come together to intercept caribou herds or disperse into smaller groups to hunt moose so they could fill their caches for winter when travel was more difficult and game less plentiful. None of these movements was random. As much as possible, people returned to the same camping places year after year.

The number of people who might live together at any one time varied depending on the season and on the task. In winter, family groups spread out but they had to make sure that each group would be able to provide for itself. Each group needed enough able-bodied adults to carry out the necessary hunting and camp work and to look after dependent members, like old people and young children. A group could not be too large: if there were misfortune or a food shortage, having to feed a large number of people could endanger the lives of everyone. Eight or ten people would be plenty to live together in winter under most circumstances.

It was also essential for each group to be mobile. To accomplish this, every group had to maintain a balance between those people who were providers and those who were dependents. Each person began life dependent on others, became a provider in adulthood, and might become dependent again in old age. A group could only move as efficiently as its slowest members. Small children and old people might have to be carried, so each group would be able to support only a limited number of dependent children and elders. A grandmother, for example, might spend one winter with one group of her children and grandchildren and another winter with another part of her family. An able-bodied man or woman might join a group that needed extra help for the winter.

At other times of the year, people might harvest resources more efficiently in larger groups. For example, salmon migrating up the

See *Part of the Land, Part of the Water*, pp 119–123 for a detailed discussion of how people came together to construct caribou surrounds. Elders talk about how different kinds of traps had to be used in different rivers. Some could be made by a single individual and others required the participation of several adults.

Johnny Johns (1898–1988). *Yukon Government photo.*

MOOSE AND CARIBOU

Johnny Johns

Johnny Johns was known as one of the top ten big game guides in the world during his career and guided hunters from Europe and the United States in the southern Yukon. In 1981, he had this to say about changing populations of moose and caribou.

I remember back in my early teens, I started hunting and there weren't too many moose then, but they multiplied quickly for some reason or another. But there were lots of caribou in those days. My dad told me that in his young days there were not so many moose but there were a lot of caribou. Funny, in the early '20s – even a little bit before that – the moose multiplied like everything. Now the moose are holding their own.

My aunt, Mrs Shorty Austin, knew how to use a snare! Her Tlingit name was *Sadusgé* and she was my mother's mother's half sister. She married that white trader, Shorty Austin.

Mrs Austin and Shorty were both too old to hunt by time I'm talking about. She took the rope off the bow of the boat – this happened up the West Arm of Lake Bennett. She saw this big bull moose track first thing, so she said, "Shorty, I'm going to snare that moose."

She was up there picking moss berries – this was the first part of August. She said Shorty just laughed at her. But she had a lot of those little bear dogs, hunting dogs, and she knew where there was a knob on the south side where the moose was staying. There was a knob up against the mountain and behind this knob was a moose trail. She knew that all the time. So she went up there and set her snare and came back down to the lake again. Then they went up there – Shorty couldn't climb; he was too old. And she took her dogs and she followed them, and sure enough there was a big bull there, caught there by the horns!

Tatshenshini River system are especially fat because their journey from the Pacific is shorter than that made by salmon ascending the Yukon River from the Bering Sea. Families would travel from considerable distances to come together in larger numbers during salmon runs. Similarly, caribou hunting differs from tracking individual moose because caribou travel in herds and are hunted most efficiently by families working cooperatively.

Game populations seem to have fluctuated in size and shifted their location during the past, and when this happened, people had to adjust too. We have already discussed how bison were driven out when the climate changed (Chapter 3).

More recent evidence of shifts in game comes from oral accounts. We are accustomed now to thinking of moose as the major large mammal in the southern Yukon and to think of caribou herds in the north. Yet both the testimonies of elders and accounts by early traders confirm that during the middle of the last century there were almost no moose in the southern Yukon and that caribou were the main large game animal. Moose must have been in the southern Yukon previously, though, because they appear in the archaeological record and Moose is a character in Mrs Kitty Smith's story about Game Mother (in *My Stories Are My Wealth*, pp 85–89).

Families were always ready to come together when food was plentiful and to spread out at other times. The key to successful hunting and fishing was this flexibility.

Bison were re-introduced into the southern Yukon during the 1980s. Attracted to the broad Shakwak Valley, they have become a traffic hazard on the north Alaska Highway during the winters of 1989 and 1990.

Material Culture: Technology and Arts

MUSEUMS tell stories too. But because they collect physical objects, they preserve certain stories and ignore others. Because museums collect "things," they encourage us to understand other cultures in terms of the physical objects they have made. Yet this emphasis on material things may say more about the societies that produce *museums* than about the societies that make the objects found in museums. Western societies pay a lot of attention to material things. People who have a lot of material objects are called "wealthy." This is a very different attitude from the one Subarctic hunting people had: for them, extra possessions were an encumbrance, slowing down travel.

Yukon material culture has sometimes been compared with that of the Pacific Northwest Coast. Visitors to museums are familiar with the arts of Northwest Coast cultures through displays of magnificent totem poles, masks and carved wooden boxes. By contrast, Yukon material culture may seem considerably less elaborate. It is not enough, though, to compare physical objects without considering reasons *why* coastal and interior material cultures may differ.

Coastal peoples were able to live in permanent villages for one major reason: they had access to an incredibly rich and reliable renewable resource. Coastal salmon runs became established at the end of the last glaciation, and these fish have since returned to the same rivers year after year, allowing people to count on their appearance every

In 1980, Mrs Angela Sidney worked with the Yukon Native Language Centre, documenting place names in Tagish and Tlingit and preparing her booklet *Place Names of the Tagish Region, Southern Yukon.* In the course of that work, she gave detailed accounts of places where she had lived and travelled as a child. Even though she is talking about the year 1912 here, she is describing a pattern of movement similar to that followed by her parents and *their* parents during the nineteenth century.

She begins by situating her account at a particular time: "This is 1912 I'm talking about, when we went to Black Lake, *T'ooch Áayi.*" She describes moving in that year with her parents and her older brother from Tagish (1) and Carcross (2) to *Taaghahi* (3), then on to Millhaven Bay (4), then to *T'ooch Áayi* (5), then back to Carcross and Tagish.

The following year, 1913, she spent the summer with her Marsh Lake cousins, camping at the foot of Marsh Lake, where the McClintock River enters that lake (6). In autumn, they moved up the lake to Judas Creek (7), then hunted up the mountain behind that creek, then crossed Marsh Lake to camp at Otter Beach, *Kooshdaa Xágu* (8), where they visited her uncle Whitehorse Billy's family before returning to Carcross. They remained there because her aunt, her father's sister, was ill.

In 1914, they went to Whitehorse (9) in March or April, then returned to Marsh Lake in summer to camp with her cousins again. By then, Angela was twelve, old enough to look after children, so she was sent to Ten Mile, *Tsuxx'aayí* (10), near Carcross, to care for her two small cousins while her uncle Patsy Henderson and his wife worked each day on their fox ranch. At the end of the summer, she returned to Marsh Lake until her father came, and they all went up the McClintock River (11) to fish camp. "I remember I felt just like I was home while I was there," she says.

That summer, they went to Whitehorse and climbed high up to Fish Lake (12), where her sixteen-year-old brother Johnny was trapping. After a brief visit, Angela and her mother took the younger children and moved back to stay with friends in the valley, near Whitehorse. In 1915, they returned to Carcross, and in the springtime Angela was "put away" in seclusion, as was customary for young women of her age.

Her account goes on, incorporating most of the 230 names for places she has mapped.

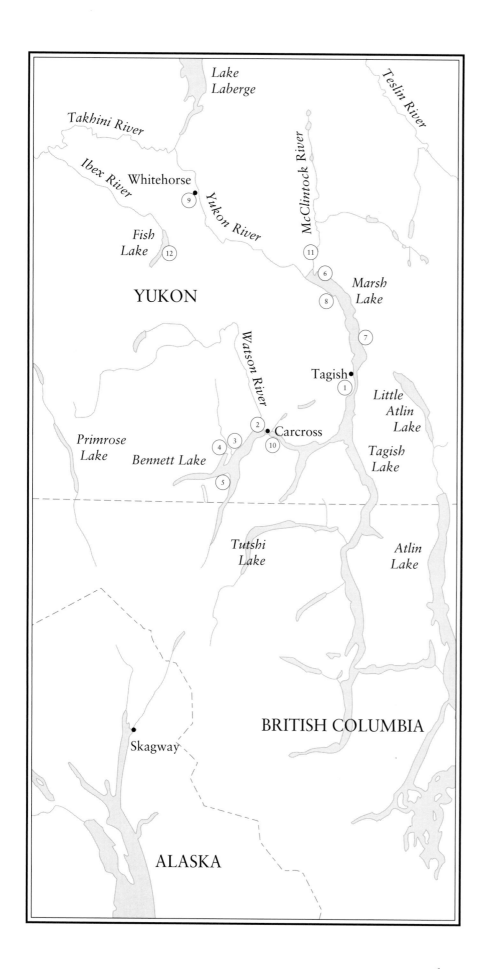

Lake
Laberge

Teslin River

Takhini River

McClintock River

Ibex River

Whitehorse
⑨

Yukon River

Fish
Lake
⑫

YUKON

⑪

⑥
⑧

Marsh
Lake

⑦

Watson River

Tagish•
①

Little
Atlin
Lake

②
Carcross
⑩

④ ③

Tagish
Lake

Primrose
Lake

Bennett Lake

⑤

Tutshi
Lake

Atlin
Lake

BRITISH COLUMBIA

•
Skagway

ALASKA

Fish camp on the Klondike River, 1898.
Photo by Tappan Adney, Yukon Archives.

Because a lot of Yukon material culture was not made to be kept, much of it did not survive. Among those artworks that have survived are wonderful pieces of women's art, recently documented in *Northern Athapaskan Art* by Kate Duncan. Working with written records, oral interviews, photographs and museum collections, Duncan has documented the intricate designs, the variations in style, and the historical changes in Yukon art styles.

summer. Halibut, sea lion and other fish and game also come within range of coastal villages each year, and shellfish are available all winter. Coastal harvesting strategies contrast sharply with those of Subarctic hunters because successful fishing requires population stability rather than mobility.

Subarctic people have always had a very different set of problems. To harvest their resources, they developed a material culture based on principles that could be combined in a variety of ways. Portability was essential. It was important to keep material baggage to a minimum so that only absolute necessities were carried from place to place. Adaptability was another principle which affected material culture. A snare, for example, can be made to trap small animals like ground squirrels, or large animals like moose and caribou. What is critical is to learn the idea of how a snare is used and the rules for how it is constructed. Then snares can be made when and where they are needed. They can be used, discarded, and made again the next time. "Wealth" in this kind of culture is carried in the head instead of on the back. It is passed on from one generation to another through oral tradition. Oral tradition is a complex and intricate art form in the Yukon. It weighs nothing and can accompany a traveller everywhere, but it does not appear in museums.

Part of the genius of Subarctic culture is the ability to take materials like bone, stone, wood, skins, bark, and copper and transform them into necessities like clothing and shelter, tools and transportation. Museums in Yukon communities provide a good place to see some of the things people have made and continue to make, and to see how this

68

is accomplished with minimal materials. Some archaeologists are working with Yukon elders to learn more about the stories that objects can tell.

Gwich'in winter house. From Alexander Murray's *Journal of the Yukon, 1847–8.*

Social Life: "Everyone Belongs"

At the foundation of nineteenth-century Yukon life is kinship and family. Throughout the world and during most of human history, people have relied heavily on family ties or kinship to structure their social organization. We now take it for granted in Canada that governments are responsible for making available a number of basic human services – health care, education, social and economic programs, and so on. Throughout human history, though, these services have more often been provided by groups of people who consider themselves to be related as part of an extended family. There are a number of different ways these relationships are traced and people from all cultures have their own ideas about family, which seem "natural" to them. One thing all kinship-based societies share is the idea that everyone has a recognized place in relation to everyone else. Everyone belongs.

The following pages give a very general outline of family organization in the southern and central Yukon. No one knows how old these traditions are, but they are probably ancient, and they continue to be important today. One way to understand this system is by outlining a few of the general rules by which it works; then we can hear it discussed by an elder who describes her experience of those rules.

Above: tanning moose hides at New Rampart House, northern Yukon. Below: tanning a moose hide in the southern Yukon. *Yukon Archives.*

The special skin tanning methods used by Yukon women were the envy of their Tlingit neighbors. Modern researchers have been unable to devise a way of duplicating this process by any commercial tanning methods. In her bilingual booklet *Dùts'ūm Edhó Ts'ètsi Yū Dän K'í/How to Tan Hides in the Native Way*, Mrs Gertie Tom describes in Tutchone and English the process by which she tans moosehides.

Rachel Dawson with her husband George and their eldest child Arthur, beside the Anglican Rectory, Fort Selkirk, about 1925. *Yukon Archives.*

In Chapter 3, Mrs Sidney tells us that at the beginning of time Crow divided people into two groups, Wolf and Crow. Anthropologists call these two divisions *moieties,* which means "halves." Membership in these two groups is determined by birth. In the Yukon you always belong to the same group as your mother; in other words, descent is *matrilineal.* By customary law, a person from one moiety can only marry someone from the opposite "side." This means that your father will always be a member of the opposite moiety from your own. Elders feel that for two Wolves to marry each other or two Crows to marry each other would be like a brother and sister marrying. In the past, such marriages were absolutely forbidden by customary law, and elders still frown on such marriages, even if the two Wolves or two Crows come from widely separated communities.

In the southern Yukon this becomes even more complicated because within each moiety there are *clans,* like *Deisheetaan* (a Crow clan), *Dakl'aweidí* (a Wolf clan), and many others. Members of any one clan can usually name a common ancestor in the distant past, though they may not always be able to trace all the steps back to that ancestor.

There are many advantages to such a system. For one thing, it gives you relatives everywhere. Even now, when young people go to visit a different community, the first question an elder is likely to ask them is, "what is your Indian name?" Because names belong to particular moieties and clans, everyone will know by the answer whether the visitor is a Wolf or Crow. The answer gives the visitor a place in that community: it tells every one *how* the visitor belongs. In the old days,

This kind of division into two groups or moieties occurs widely throughout the world. Although descent is traced through the mother's line in the Yukon, this is not the case everywhere; in other cultures the father's side may determine one's membership in a moiety; and in still others, both sides receive equal emphasis.

THE LAST BIG POTLATCH

Rachel Dawson

For a detailed discussion of potlatches in the Yukon, see *Part of the Land, Part of the Water*, pp 215–222.

The last big potlatch was in 1914, in Fort Selkirk. It was for my grandmother.

Those days, boy, you should see the stuff they give away! Maybe fifty 30.30 Winchester guns. People came from Big Lake (Aishihik) and all over. Wolf people. My grandmother was Crow. Crow people gave to Wolf people (to pay them back for helping at the funeral).

Crow people feed Wolf people too. They don't buy one pound of grub for themselves! Wolf people eat first. Now they mix everything up at potlatches, but at that time only the Wolf people ate [if the potlatch was given to thank them]. Crows would eat their grub at home. They're not supposed to eat at the potlatch when they're the ones putting it up.

Before they give stuff away, they sang that song, "Crying song." Instead of crying when a person dies, you sing to them. They do a dance, wear button blankets. They wore hats with lots of ribbons on them. Women had long hair. They all did that kind of dance. They're not happy when they're doing it — sort of sad, sour looking. Then after it is all over, everybody changed again. They took those hats off and put them on Wolf people's heads. Then they cut the button blankets in half and gave them to Wolf people. Just Wolf people get them. They gave away Hudson Bay blankets too — tear them in half and give them to Wolf women, Wolf men — they all get that. They packed everything away. They gave away cups and plates and everything. They gave guns to the men. They piled up moose skins too, about fifty — piled them up about eight times. People took about two or three packs home.

Just Wolf people got those things, because they did all the work for the funeral. When my grandma died they just made a little tea and invited people. And then they waited for one year to put up her fence. That's the time they had the big party and made a collection.

---

this system helped people to establish important friendships and even partnerships with other groups through marriage ties. In an area as large as the Yukon, where groups were widely spread out, it was important to have networks of friends and relations that cut across small family groups. Given the variability of resources it is especially important for hunters to have family they could depend on in a number of places. In the next chapter we will see how important this was for trade.

Matrilineal descent was reinforced by another custom, which encouraged a man to live with his wife's family after marriage, at least for a while. He would hunt in partnership with her brother, and they might exchange trade goods with each other. A man would also be responsible for looking after his wife's parents in their old age. As long

GETTING MARRIED

Rachel Dawson

In those days, a girl's mother chooses her husband. If two people are to get married, their families decide. Then everybody in the camp has a big meeting. If someone disagrees, they say so. Just like now in church, if you don't think people should marry, you say it right there; you don't complain later. Those people would talk about it. One bunch might not like it. The other bunch might think it's okay and tell the first bunch to be quiet. Wolf and Crow, they argue like this.

When people get married, we don't kick them out like white people. We bring them in here. If my daughter marries a man, he moves in here. I teach him how to get meat, how to put up food. When they're trained, then you let them go.

If a Wolf and a Wolf marry, or if a Crow and a Crow marry, people have no respect for them or for their kids. A long time ago, they used to kill people if they broke that law.

Those kinds of marriages in the early days were faithful: I told my grandchildren, "You should let me choose your husband or your wife for you! Don't fall in love like your white brother or sister, or the person you marry may leave." I tell those kids they are Wolf, because their mother is Wolf. Me, I'm Crow and my son is Crow so he married a woman who is Wolf and those kids are Wolf. Those kids have to marry Crow, not Wolf. My mother didn't plan my marriage though. Me, I did like my white sister and brother!

Mr Dawson and I met when we were kids, when his father and mother came from Lake Laberge to Fort Selkirk. . . . Later we met again when I was seventeen. He was working on the steamboat then. I met him after school. We got acquainted. He went back home and later he wrote and said he wanted to marry me. We were married July 28, 1923. We lived down there at Fort Selkirk until my mother died in 1927. Then we moved up here.

Mrs Rachel Dawson was born in 1902 and passed away in 1976. Between 1974 and 1976, when she recorded her life story, she had this to say about marriage customs.

as they continued living with her family, she would be able to work with her mother and sisters, and these women might raise their children together.

Living with the woman's family after marriage had other benefits. A man would get to know two hunting areas well: the one where he was raised and his wife's. A woman would have very detailed knowledge of berry grounds and the locations of vegetable roots. Women's knowledge could be critical during a particularly difficult winter when meat was scarce. The detailed knowledge women had about their local areas must have had great importance during the bitterly cold years of the "Little Ice Age" just prior to the coming of the first whites.

Kinship, then, works as a kind of map that tells a person where he or she belongs in a social world and also on the land.

This song was made by Copper Lily Johnson, a Crow, for her Wolf husband, Jimmy Johnson, sometime in the 1940s. "They were just married. She should sing love song to him," Mrs Annie Ned laughs. Instead, she makes affectionate fun of him. The result has become one of the most popular First Nations songs in the southern Yukon, and there are now many versions. This one was recorded by Mrs Ned in 1983.

Jimmy Johnson-ah,　　　*mekeshäna*　*daghwäda.*
Jimmy Johnson-ah,　　　your foot bones　are crooked.

Nidaw　*izhüra.*　　　　*Dadǫą*　　　*nintläla.*
For you　I did it.　　　　You come back　you are hopping
　　　　　　　　　　　　toward us　　　along.

Wezat k'aya　　　　　*daghwäda,*　*ahayahay.*
Your shin bones　　　　are crooked.

Naghaya　*lach'ia*　　*mekeshäna*　*daghwäda.*
Wolverine looks like,　　your foot bones　are crooked.

A fairly literal translation, carrying through all four verses, goes like this:

Jimmy Johnson, Jimmy Johson,
your foot bones are crooked. I did it for you.
Ahayahaoo.

Jimmy Johnson, Jimmy Johnson,
you come back hopping. I did it for you.
Your foot bones are crooked. Ahayahaya, ahayahaya.

Jimmy Johnson, Jimmy Johnson,
you come back hopping. I did it for you.
Your shin bones are crooked. Ahayahaya, ahayahaya.

Jimmy Johnson, Jimmy Johnson,
you come back hopping. I did it for you.
Ahayahaoo.
Just like a wolverine's, your foot bones are bent.

But when Mrs Ned translates the song into English, she interprets it this way:

Jimmy Johnson-ah,
I cook for you, I boil meat for you.
Your legs are crooked!

1-4. Jim - my John - son - ah, Jim - my John - son - ah,

1. me - kesh - ä - na da - ghwäda ni - daw i - (i) - zhüra,
2 - 3. da - (a) - do̱ - a̱ nin - tlä - la, ni - daw i - (i) - zhüra,
4. ni - (i) - daw i - (i) - zhüra, da - do̱ - a̱ nin - tlä - la,

1.

1. a - ha - ya - ha - oo - oo.

2. & 3.

2. me - kesh - ä - na da - ghwä - da, a - hi - ya -
3. we - zat k'a - ya da - ghwä - da, a - hi - ya -

2 - 3. hi - ya u - a - hi - ya - hi - ya.

4.

4. a - ha - ya - ha - oo - oo,

4. na - ghaya - la - ch'ia o - we - kesh - ä - na da - ghwäda.

Trapping for trade. Note the indigenous
snare, along with the imported rifle,
pipe and clothing. *Yukon Archives.*

The Fur Trade 5

THE FUR TRADE is often discussed in history books as though it were a distinct *period* in Canadian history, as though it were an event or a series of events that occurred at some time in the past, and then stopped. But in the North, trapping is an activity which began long before Europeans arrived. And trapping for furs continues to have social and economic importance in many communities. It is not a chapter of history that began and ended at some point in the past.

Indigenous people relied on fur bearing animals for food, clothing and shelter long before the European-based fur trade began, of course. Beaver, for example, were originally hunted as much for their meat as for their hides. But as competing traders came to the coast of north-western North America from Russia and from Britain, the reasons people trapped began shifting from the *use* value of those furs to their *exchange* value. Beaver pelts became an important exchange item once it was discovered that the fine guard hairs were excellent for making fabric used in men's hats.

The fur trade has been important in the northern economy for so long that it dominates the history of the late nineteenth century. Furs were the marketable resource that first drew outsiders to the North. Because those outsiders brought with them a range of goods to exchange for furs, trapping for trade gradually became a central activity for people living on the Yukon Plateau. Today, when elders talk about the traditional way of life, they are usually referring to a time when the fur trade was already well established.

At the time when European trading companies began competing with each other for furs, indigenous peoples in Canada had distinct and well-established forms of government and economy. The fur trade was the first industry to link them with European economies, and this connection usually had greater benefits for the Europeans than for the aboriginal people.

A great deal has been written about the fur trade, but because writers on this subject ask different questions, they come to quite different conclusions.

Historians and economists, for example, write about the fur trade as a market-oriented *business*. They investigate the problems involved in the collection and transportation of furs from northern communities to urban centres. They look for linkages between fur production in Canada and fur markets in Russia, Britain and the United States. Their emphasis is on the fur trade as an industry and their concern is to demonstrate how this fits into large-scale industrial economies.

The history of frontier trade throughout the world shows that everywhere the non-urban peoples nearest the trading centre sought to bar other "natives" from direct access to the metropolitan trade and that they used their possession of superior arms, obtained in trade, to maintain their middleman position. . . . Such motives and means played an important part in the post-Columbian history of the American Indians. . . .
– Richard Slobodin, *Band Organization of the Peel River Kutchin*, p 23

Well, Coast Indians came in here a long time before white people. People had fur, and they used it for everything themselves. Nobody knows alcohol, nobody knows sugar before those Coast Indians came. They brought guns, too. No white man here, nothing.
– Mrs Annie Ned

Three manuscripts discussing nineteenth century Yukon fur trade are available in the Yukon Archives. Two are based on extensive discussion with Yukon elders and the third analyzes historical records.

In "Culture Change and Native Trade in the Southern Yukon Territory," completed in 1950, Catharine McClellan discusses trade relationships between Tlingit people on the coast and Tagish, Southern Tutchone and Inland Tlingit people in the southern Yukon. Adrian Tanner's manuscript "The Structure of Fur Trade Relations" was written in 1965, based on discussions with trappers in Pelly Crossing and Carmacks and his own investigations of how the fur trade operated in this region. A more recent manuscript by Ken Coates, "Furs Along the Yukon," is based on an analysis of fur trade records and gives considerable detail about trade in the northern Yukon.

The interest of Yukon archaeologists in oral tradition is summed up by William Workman who has done detailed archaeological investigation in the southern Yukon at Aishihik. Referring to the nineteenth-century trade which dominated Tlingit-Athapaskan relationships, he points out that oral tradition contributes as much evidence as the archaeological record:

It is humbling to realize how much this transforming trade was carried on in perishables and how scanty the archaeological record for it is, in view of its documented significance. Almost invariably we will underestimate the volume of trade in the prehistoric record of this area, given the likelihood that much of it was also in perishable items. . . .

See Workman's *Prehistory of the Aishihik-Kluane Area, Southwest Yukon,* p 94

Anthropologists, on the other hand, usually focus on how Native people have participated in the fur trade as *producers*. They look at the actual work done by men and women engaged in trapping and preparing furs, the kinds of exchanges made by trappers, the way trappers organize their production of furs until those furs reach the trader. They look at the effects the fur trade has had on Native families, subsistence economies and political organization.

Somewhere between these two approaches is a third approach. We might look at how the social relations between people actually involved in the exchange of furs have changed over time. Some of the evidence about these changes is available from written records; some comes from oral accounts.

In the nineteenth century, we can distinguish three phases of trade. First, the earliest arrangements for trade were through *aboriginal trade networks*, based on cultural understandings that had built up over many generations. Second, the arrival of the first white traders in the 1840s, representatives of the *Hudson's Bay Company*, caused some changes to longstanding patterns. Third, by the 1870s *independent American traders* were arriving on the Yukon River, and they in turn had different ideas about how trade should be conducted.

Aboriginal Trade Networks

LONG BEFORE the arrival of European traders in northwestern North America, a flourishing trade existed between coastal and interior communities. The outlines of this aboriginal trade are hazy because the earliest trade items – skins, seaweed, oil – were perishable and rarely survive in the archaeological record. This makes it difficult to estimate how long that trade had gone on. One of the most important aspects of this early trade was the opportunity it provided for social contacts. Consequently, it should not be surprising that archaeologists have turned to oral evidence to fill in some of the gaps in the material record.

If we were to rely on written records alone for our understanding of aboriginal trade, we might never hear about places like Aishihik, Hutshi or Noogaayík in the southwest Yukon. Yet these are the names elders mention repeatedly when they talk about the trading centres which were important in their childhood. Most travellers who wrote during the late nineteenth century followed the conventional river routes, never visiting the centres where aboriginal trappers walked to trade.

Trade is especially likely to occur between groups of people who live in areas that are geographically distinct and where resources differ. In such a situation, people can exchange plentiful staples for foods and materials that are not locally available. Athapaskan people living on the central Yukon Plateau were separated by mountains from Coastal Tlingit in the southwest and from Arctic Inuit in the north. In each case, coastal peoples were able to exchange products from the sea for skins and furs from the interior high country. In the southwestern Yukon, for example, three Tlingit tribes – the Chilkat, Chilkoot and

Taku – made annual trips to the interior to trade, bringing dried fish, eulachon oil, shell ornaments and cedar bark baskets to exchange for caribou hides, moccasins, fur garments and native copper. In the north, Gwich'in middlemen brought oil, bone and tusks from the Arctic coast and made similar exchanges with inland people.

During this early period one of the most common ways to organize trading relationships was through partnerships between traders from different cultural groups. Family ties also made trade partnerships stronger and more permanent. In a partnership between an Athapaskan man and a Tlingit man, for example, families sometimes arranged for one partner to marry the other partner's sister. Mrs Annie Ned, born at Hutshi, talks about her grandfather's long time trading partner, Gasłeeni. She and her brother continue to maintain Gasłeeni's grave as a sign of respect for that alliance.

Partnerships were even more formalized in the north because of longstanding hostilities between coastal Inuit and interior Gwich'in peoples. A partnership between two men from potentially hostile groups was invaluable. Partners were responsible for protecting one another even if a conflict arose between their respective communities.

Whether trappers were taking furs for their own use or for trade, they always had a clear understanding about their relationship with the animals whose furs they took. Mrs Kitty Smith begins and concludes her story of "The Man Who Stayed with Groundhog" with clear instructions about how people should behave when they trap. The story concerns a man who trapped groundhogs and mistreated the carcasses, casting them carelessly in the fire. The Groundhog Spirit decided that the man should be put in a situation where he could understand how his foolish actions put the relationship between *all* humans and animals at risk. Groundhogs enticed him to their world where he began to see things through their eyes and to understand the consequences of human arrogance. Later, when he returned to his own people, he made a speech telling them about his thoughtless behavior so that they could all learn from his experience. These rules continue to bind animals and humans today.

Many people in the southern Yukon discuss the responsibilities involved in such a partnership by telling a narrative about "Falling Through the Glacier." It tells how two partners, one Athapaskan, one Tlingit, were crossing a glacier as they travelled from the interior to the coast. Unexpectedly, the Tlingit man fell into an ice crevasse. The story dramatizes the responsibilities involved in a partnership. One version, told by Mrs Sidney, appears in her *Tagish Tlaagú*, p 88; a version by Mrs Kitty Smith is in *Nindal Kwädindür*, pp 95–7; Mrs Ned tells the narrative in her booklet, *Old People in those Days, They Told Their Story all the Time*, pp 52–55.

For versions of this narrative told by Mrs Smith and by Mrs Angela Sidney, see *My Stories Are My Wealth*, pp 53–57.

A Chilkat Tlingit man on a trading expedition. Engraving by F. Unte, published by Aurel Krause in 1885.

Annie Ned

At Noogaayík [a nineteenth-century fishing village on the Tatshenshini River], Tlingit people first saw chips floating down from upriver. People making rafts, I guess, and the chips floated down.

"Where did this one come from?" they asked. So that time Coast Indians went in wintertime to Dalton Post. That's the way they met these Yukon Indians. Yukon people are hunting, and they've got nice skin clothes — oh, gee, porcupine quills, moose skins, moccasins! Everything nice.

Coast Indians saw those clothes and they wanted them! That's the way they found out about these Yukon people. Right then, they found where we hunted. Coast Indians traded them knives, axes, and they got clothes, babiche, fish skin from the Yukon. They've got *nothing,* those Tlingit people, just cloth clothes, groundhog clothes. Nothing! Goat and groundhog, that's all.

But people here had lots of fur and they used it in everything themselves — ready-made moccasins, buckskin parky [parka], silver fox, red fox, caribou skin parky sewed up with porcupine quills. You can't see it this time [any more], that kind. I saw it, that time. My grandma got it . . . so pretty. . . .

So that's how they got it! Coast Indians got snowshoes and moose skin clothes — all warm — parky, caribou parky, caribou blanket, caribou mattress. Anything like that they want to use. Those people wanted clothes from here in Yukon . . . skin clothes, sheepskin, warm mitts . . . so they traded. They did it for a purpose. Our grandpas make different snowshoes in this Yukon. They fixed them with caribou skin babiche, nice snowshoes. Coast Indians traded for snowshoes, traded for clothes. They traded for snowshoe string, for babiche, for sinew, for tanned skin — all soft.

I don't know the time Coast Indians came to this Yukon. My grandmother, my grandpa, *they* told me that's the way.

These Yukon people told Coast Indians to come back in summertime. So they did, next summer. Yukon people had lots of furs. That time they don't know money — they don't know where to sell them. So Coast Indians brought in guns. Well, they're surprised about that, Yukon people! They've been using bow and arrow! So they traded.

Coast Indians got guns, knives, axes. They came on snowshoes. They packed sugar, tea, tobacco, cloth to sew. Rich people would have eight packers each! They brought shells, they brought anything to trade. They traded for clothes. Coast Indians brought sugar, tea. At first these Yukon people didn't want it. . . . But people here got crazy for it [trade goods]. They traded for knives, they traded for anything, they say — shells, guns, needles. When you buy that gun, you've got to pile up furs how long is that gun, same as that gun, how tall! Then you get that gun.

Mrs Annie Ned was born sometime during the 1890s at the old settlement of Hutshi in the southern Yukon Territory. Her mother, *Tùtałma,* was a woman of the Crow moiety from the Dalton Post region, and her father, *Sakuni,* was one of six sons of the man known as the Hutshi Chief. Mrs Ned spent her childhood around Hutshi and most of her adult years near Kusawa Lake and the Takhini River system. She remains a powerful figure in southern Yukon society and is known as a person having special knowledge about spiritual power. Underlying this knowledge is her clear understanding about the power of words, the importance of using words carefully, and the consequences of speaking publicly about things one should not discuss. Mrs Ned was awarded the Order of Canada in 1990 for her contributions to maintaining and teaching the songs, dances and oral histories of her people. *Yukon Government photo, 1990.*

The Arrival of European Traders

P RIOR TO 1840, the central part of what is now the Yukon Territory was used exclusively by Athapaskan and Tlingit-speaking peoples. The commercial fur trade that came to affect aboriginal peoples on the Yukon River was driven by forces from outside the Yukon and developed from two different directions. Russian traders came from the west and British traders from the east. Both were originally drawn to the Pacific Northwest Coast by the trade in sea otter furs.

The European fur market, though, had no limits. There were never enough furs arriving at posts to satisfy the demands in Moscow, Leningrad, London and Paris. The pressures put on that trade were impossible to sustain, and by the mid 1800s, sea otters were all but exterminated on the coast. Without pausing to consider the implications of this, trading companies turned their attention beyond the mountains to the interior.

The Russian American Company had a post at Sitka shortly after 1800. Russian traders came into immediate contact with Tlingit tribes who already knew about furs beyond the St Elias Mountains. Tlingits, in turn, saw considerable advantage in firmly establishing their position as middlemen in trade between Europeans and inland peoples. They did so by claiming exclusive control of the only three mountain passes between the coast and interior. These passes then came to be named for the Tlingit tribes that controlled them – the Chilkat, the Chilkoot and Taku passes. Tlingit traders simply refused to allow Europeans to travel inland, and European traders saw that their only choice was to take advantage of the existing networks. Writing in 1885, the German ethnographer Aurel Krause noted,

Aurel Krause, *The Tlingit Indians*, p 137

A visit on the part of a white man to the Athapaskans to trade with them directly was regarded by the Chilkat as an infringement of their rights and likely to be prevented by force. Just as every tribe had its hunting and fishing territory, so they had their trading trails; the Chilkat went up the Chilkat River, the Chilkoot over the Chilkoot Pass and it took lengthy negotiations to reverse the procedure.

Further east, on the other side of the Cordillera, a different kind of competition was occurring between trading companies as they worked their way across northern North America trying to secure reliable supplies of fur. The Northwest Company had reached Fort Good Hope by 1805, and in their amalgamation with the Hudson's Bay Company in 1821, they acquired the name, privileges and charter of the old Hudson's Bay Company. Between 1805 and 1840, the British who were based east of the Cordillera saw the area now called the Yukon as a kind of buffer zone between themselves and the Russians on the coast. As far as we know, neither Russian nor British traders actually reached the upper Yukon River during these years. Instead they continued to rely on middlemen in the established aboriginal trade networks – Gwich'in in the north and Tlingit in the south – to bring furs out to their posts.

At the same time, international agreements were affecting trading strategies. In 1825, the 141st meridian was established as the boundary between British and Russian America. In 1839, the British leased what is now southeastern Alaska from Russia. This gave the Hudson's Bay Company much greater control over Yukon furs because now, in addition to trading overland through their eastern posts, they were able to send ships to the coast. There, they adopted the same strategy the Russians had, working through the Tlingit trade networks and purchasing furs from the Tlingits. From the east, though, the Hudson's Bay Company began a cautious two-pronged exploration into the territory. This was partly to find out what existed in this enormous area of land they considered "unexplored," and partly to try to head off competition from Russian traders on the lower Yukon River.

In the north, John Bell travelled up the Peel River. Alexander Murray followed him in 1847 and continued to the mouth of the Porcupine where it joins the Yukon. There, he built Fort Yukon. In the southeast, John McLeod travelled up the Frances River. Robert Campbell later followed the same route and carried on to explore the Pelly River. All of these men had Native guides, but only Campbell made regular mention of them in reports – Lapie, Ketza and his interpreter Francis Hoole. The Hudson's Bay Company had established a post on Dease Lake by 1838, on Frances Lake by 1842, at Pelly Banks by 1846 and then at Fort Selkirk by 1848.

The posts on the Francis and Pelly Rivers were never very successful and they closed within a few years. But when Campbell first reached the mouth of the Pelly River where it enters the Yukon, he was astounded by the levels of trading activity already established there between Tlingits and Athapaskans. Writing to his headquarters on 25 July 1843, he predicted that he would have trouble breaking into this trade network. The picture he describes is one of abundant food and trade goods and considerable time for festivities. Campbell established Fort Selkirk there in 1848, aware that by doing so he was offending the Tlingit traders. Writing to his superiors at Fort Simpson three years later, in October of 1851, Campbell reported nervously about the relative ineffectiveness of his post. A few months later, in August 1852, the Chilkat traders came inland and destroyed Fort Selkirk because it interfered with their trade monopoly on the Yukon River.

For years, Tlingits had collected furs from the Yukon River and carried them out to the coast to sell, first to Russians, then to British traders. By making trade goods directly available to people who already had an established place in the Tlingit network, Campbell was directly challenging a well-established monopoly. Tlingit traders found this totally unacceptable and destroyed his post for that reason.

Generally, the Hudson's Bay Company followed a rule that cultural practices should be disrupted as little as possible. This was not because of high-minded intentions; their motives were far simpler. The HBC had a virtual monopoly on Yukon furs after 1848: whether furs were brought directly to the post by trappers or whether they came via Gwich'in or Tlingit middlemen, they ended up in HBC hands. The Company reasoned that the less they disrupted longstanding social

Gwich'in people dancing. From Alexander Murray's *Journal of the Yukon, 1847–8*.

relationships in Native communities, the more likely they were to maximize their own profits.

In the northern Yukon, the Hudson's Bay Company did introduce one change by appointing "trading chiefs" who were delegated to deal directly with the H B C trader. The trading chief was expected to be in charge of the business of collecting furs from other trappers, bargaining with the trader, and distributing the trade goods to trappers. A trading chief was given symbols of power – special clothes or trade goods – by the trader. Then that trading chief managed the business of trade. The trader simply located his post in a convenient place and the aboriginal trading system carried on much as in the past. Trading chiefs were particularly important in the north at Fort McPherson, La Pierre House, and Fort Yukon.

The nineteenth-century fur industry was based on ideas of fashion characteristic of a particular historical period in Europe. First beaver hats, then fur stoles and muffs, later fur coats made Yukon furs a valuable commodity because of their scarcity, cost and durability. But Europeans were not the only people interested in fashion, as we see from some of the beautiful decorative work done by Yukon women.

Traders in the field are sometimes portrayed as callous exploiters exchanging "beads and trinkets" for more valuable furs. Yet Campbell (and other traders) repeatedly complained that trappers had their own very specific ideas about items they were willing to accept in trade, and refused to trade until they got what they wanted. Writing in 1843, he noted, "One thing is for certain that the young men must have their ornaments to decorate themselves for their festive dances . . . and that

84

is what they'll use their furs for . . ." (HBC B/200/b/17, p 16). Hudson's Bay Company records show how traders had to scramble to keep up with a rapidly changing and competitive market in beads as Athapaskan men and women bargained carefully for particular sizes, shapes and colors.

Women experimented with designs made possible by new varieties of beads. Artistic traditions in these regions became more elaborate as women began working with different colors and textures, integrating new designs – floral patterns, especially – into established traditions. Ideas of beauty, fashion and art, then, may have influenced the fur trade from several traditions, both Native and European. If furs fueled a European fashion industry, the trade seems also to have fostered an indigenous artistic tradition in northern Canada.

Even today, Athapaskan and Tlingit women are able to recognize where a beaded moccasin, glove or jacket comes from – and even identify the artist – by the design, the kind of beads, the size of the flowers, the pattern followed.

Remains of Fort Selkirk in 1883. The engraving was made from a photograph taken by Frederick Schwatka in that year, published in Schwatka's *Along Alaska's Great River.*

In her recent book on decorative arts in northwestern North America, *Northern Athapaskan Art: a Beadwork Tradition,* Kate Duncan documents the elaborate artistic traditions that developed during the period of intensive fur trade in the Yukon, Northwest Territories, Alaska and northern British Columbia.

A typescript of Campbell's daily journal, entitled Two Journals of Robert Campbell, *is available at the Yukon Archives and makes fascinating reading. The quotations included here, though, come from letters Campbell wrote to the Hudson's Bay headquarters at Fort Simpson, and those he received in return. In his letters, Campbell reported that the people at the forks of the Pelly and Yukon Rivers were extremely well situated. They had plenty of food and seemed to have lots of time to trade. His handwritten letters describe the scene in his own words. The people he met, he said, had*

Campbell writing on 23 July 1843. HBC Archives B/200/b/17, p 16

belts or bands of these beads at least 4 or 5 lbs and of some yards long . . . which they use for dances demonstrated by people at the Forks [of Pelly and Yukon Rivers] who have a lot of such dances . . . a pastime of which they are passionately fond and in which they no doubt often indulge as they appear from various circumstances and also from such large parties being always together to be strangers to the want of food so common on this side of the mountains, a good inducement to promote merrisome [times?] and merry making.

But on 18 October 1851, Campbell wrote to Fort Simpson:

Hudson's Bay Company correspondence B/200/b/29, p 236

I am sorry to report that a large party (31) of trading Indians from the coast who visited the Pelly and remained here 'til they got their loads traded made a clean sweep of all of the furs and leather of the surrounding vicinity. Some of the same Indians even went down the river near a hundred miles. This long established traffic, the very low price at which they dispose their goods, and their acquaintance with the language and the habits of these tribes afford them facilities for trade we are all deprived of. . . .

On 8 January 1852, James Anderson replied from Fort Simpson:

HBC correspondence B/200/b/29, p 24

As far as I can judge from the very imperfect information I have received, Selkirk is placed too near the coast; you will be troubled by the incurrences of the Indian traders from the coast who can dispose of their goods at a far cheaper rate than we can afford to sell ours. It strikes me forcibly that were the post from 60 to 100 miles down the river, it would be better situated for trade and more out of the sphere of these traders. It would also have the effect of drawing the Indians below. You appear to have seen numerous bands of Indians lower down the river and it is highly probable from that circumstance that the country is rich both in large animals and furs.

On 20 August 1852, a party of 27 Chilkats arrived, this time intent on more than underselling Campbell's post. "I was dragged and pushed toward the bank," Campbell reports,

HBC correspondence B/200/b/29, p 167

one only of those holding my arms warded off several knife thrusts, and I believe under Providence I owe my life to so many having hold of me. . . . In the struggle I felt sure of death. . . .

86

It is interesting to compare oral and written accounts of this event. For example, Mrs Rachel Dawson, born at Fort Selkirk, heard an account of the same event from her mother's father. She says that her grandfather was given the English name Campbell by Robert Campbell because he was the man who actually saved the trader's life:

My grandfather, my mother's father, got his name from the Hudson Bay man Robert Campbell. That time when the Alaska Indians came to burn down his post, my grandpa saved him. He hid him and tied him to a boat and pushed him out into the river. So he saved his life.

At that time, Indians had no whiteman name. So Robert Campbell said to my grandpa, "Because you saved me, you have my name."

My grandpa tried to tell him to come back [to Fort Selkirk]. But Robert Campbell, the white man, was afraid. So my grandpa Campbell gave him some dry fish. That Hudson Bay man went away and he never came back. I guess maybe he went to build a post somewhere else.

We learn from the written record that Robert Campbell walked thousands of miles, first to Fort Simpson, and then to Minnesota to try to convince his superiors, particularly Governor Simpson, to retaliate against the Chilkats and to resupply his Yukon post. The Company had already decided, though, that the Yukon operation was unprofitable, and Campbell never returned to the Yukon.

Years later, in 1898, a Northwest Mounted Police Officer named Jarvis visited the community of Klukwan, Alaska, and the Tlingit chief there showed him a flag they had taken from Fort Selkirk and kept as a statement of their resistance to white encroachment. Jarvis described it as

an old flag of the "British Columbia Company" eighteen by twenty-four feet, so old that it would almost fall to pieces. This flag was taken from the company's post at Fort Selkirk in 1852, when the post was raided, plundered and burned down by the Chilkats, headed by the present chief's father.

A. M. Jarvis, Annual Report, 31 October 1898, p 104

Beadwork in the Athapaskan style (this page) and Tlingit style (facing page). *McBride Museum, Whitehorse. Yukon Government photo.*

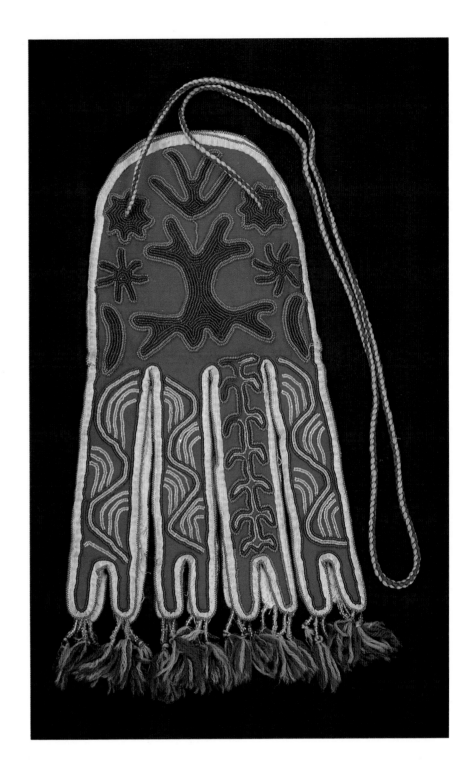

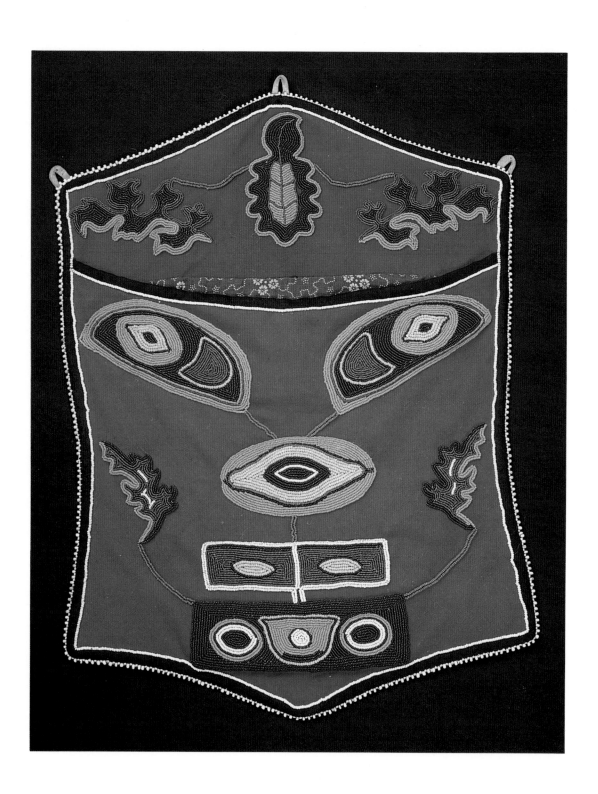

Some Early Yukon Trading Posts and Camps

Independent Traders

AFTER THE EXPULSION of the Hudson's Bay Company, aboriginal trade continued, much as in the past, with additional European trade goods reaching the Yukon River from distant posts. By the 1870s, other pressures, again from outside the Yukon, were signalling a new phase of trade. Rumours of mineral wealth on the Yukon River were drawing increasing numbers of white prospectors, government officials and trappers to this area. Tlingits were finding it extremely difficult to retain their monopoly control of the passes from coast to interior by the 1880s.

As the Tlingit monopoly declined, individual prospectors were managing to cross the mountains from the coast. One of the early traders who successfully challenged the Tlingit blockade was Jack Dalton, an American cowboy with a taste for adventure. His trip to the Yukon in 1890 is well documented because he came with a journalist named E. J. Glave, who was sponsored by *Frank Leslie's Illustrated Newspaper* in New York to write about his travels "in the interior of Alaska." Glave's written accounts (available at the Yukon Archives) are illustrated with detailed drawings of people and places. When Catharine McClellan brought copies of some of these sketches to Haines Junction in the 1970s, elders were able to identify by name some of the people Glave had drawn eighty years before.

Others besides Jack Dalton came to the Yukon for adventure and saw that trading could be a profitable business. Several of them set up posts to trade with both Native trappers and white prospectors. Arthur Harper, Leroy Napoleon McQuesten, and Albert Mayo traded at various points on the Yukon River system. By 1900, with increasing competition, there were posts within range of all Yukon trappers.

These traders saw little advantage in working within established trade networks or through trading chiefs. Instead, they imported a system used in the American West, called "jawbone," a term still used by elderly Yukon trappers. A trader would extend credit to an individual trapper, supplying him with the provisions he needed, on condition that the trapper would bring all his furs back to the same trader. The "jawbone" system, based on credit and debt, probably had more dislocating effects on fur production than any trading method used up to that point. By labelling some trappers as "better risks" than others for credit, this system emphasized new distinctions between people. A good trapper was pleased to have a large "jawbone," but it also put him in debt to a particular trader. Such arrangements gave the trader more power than the trapper to decide what furs should be trapped. This imbalance increased as trappers became increasingly dependent on consumer goods which they could acquire only by trapping whichever furs were bringing good prices that year.

More recent changes go beyond the scope of this book, but if we were to continue to discuss the fur trade in the twentieth century we would need to look at additional influences. Serious pressure on animal populations began to occur in some parts of the Yukon shortly after the gold rush, when some prospectors decided to stay on as

Sketches by E. J. Glave of people he met in the Yukon in 1890. Glave recorded the name of the man below as "Gunar Arcku."

Jack Dalton, leading a horse on snowshoes, about 1890. *Photo by E. J. Glave. University of Alaska Archives.*

JACK DALTON POST

Kitty Smith

Jack Dalton established his trading post, called Dalton Post, in the 1890s, when Mrs Kitty Smith was just a small girl. Ninety years later, in the 1980s, she recalled his arrival.

I know when Jack Dalton first came in. I was raised at Dalton Post. Jack Dalton, he's got a store there – that's why "Jack Dalton Post" they call it. He brought working people with him, Indians. These people are Telegraph [Tahltan] Indians, but they speak Tlingit. My grandma knows what they're saying: they told her where they came from. Jack Dalton was a big shot! He had about twenty-five working people.

They built two buildings, one warehouse, one store. I used to buy raisins at his store. He married an Indian woman – did you know that? He's got one kid, but that kid died. This wife died too. . . . After that, he went outside. Since that, he never came back. I guess he might come back some day. . . .

They've got no money at Dalton Post – just tickets: red one is one dollar; yellow is twenty-five cents, two bits; blue one is fifty cents. That's just how far they got – three. In Haines they used real money, but not at Jack Dalton Post. Yes, I know the time Jack Dalton came.

trappers. By 1908, a geologist named Joseph Keele reported that $136,000 worth of furs had been taken from the Pelly and Macmillan river country during the previous five years. He compared the methods of white trappers with those of Native trappers: the former arrived with provisions, built a cabin and trapped intensively in one area until all the furs were gone; the latter "seldom trap a locality out, as they are forced to move their camps often in search of game, and consequently trap lightly over a large area." His comments were echoed by Poole Field, a trader on the Pelly from 1903–1913, who observed of Native trappers that

they are continually on the move, only stopping a few days in one place, and cover a large tract of country in a year. Their food supply is taken from such a large country that it leaves plenty to breed from, so although an Indian kills a lot of game in the year he does the country very little harm.

Elders have expressed mixed views about how the fur trade affected the lives of people in the Yukon. Their perspectives also take into account changes in the fur trade during the twentieth century. Over time, new trade items like dogs, canvas tents, and wire snares all altered the kinds of work families had to do to produce furs and the way they organized these activities. Competition from outsiders meant that trappers had a more restricted land base on which to trap. The registration of traplines by governments disrupted customary moiety, clan and family trapping patterns. More recently, the activities of animal rights groups have affected trapping economies across the north.

Speaking in the 1970s, John Joe, a Southern Tutchone elder, said,

I used to lose money at it [fur trading] so it's no good. Sometimes the less they give me I tell them, "go hunt your own fur." A lot of times we know it was pretty low, but we just let it go because we've got no place else to go.

On balance, though, trappers were able to maintain control of their lives as long as fur prices remained relatively stable, and prices for Yukon furs were consistently high well into the twentieth century. In 1970 elder Jimmy Joe from Kluane Lake recalled his childhood at Burwash post:

In the old days, people had better living, better times than they have today. In the old days, people hunt and trap starting in November . . . December . . . January . . . February. For four months, they trap. They come in with furs. . . . They sell the furs. They buy what little they want at the trading post. Then they have a good time. . . . No drinking in those days. . . . It is the spring of the year.

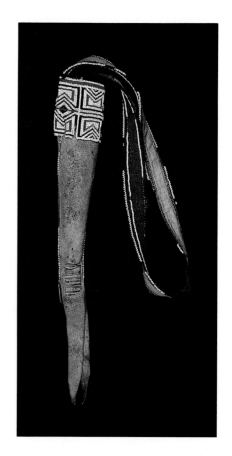

Beaded scabbard, found on Herschel Island, undated. *McBride Museum, Whitehorse. Yukon Government photo.*

For a discussion of the Yukon fur trade between 1900 and 1950, see Robert McCandless, *Yukon Wildlife*, University of Alberta Press, 1985. This quotation from John Joe is taken from p 163 of McCandless's book.

The Drummer.

285. Men's English black beaver cloth overcoats, 50 inches long, lined with natural dark muskrat, faced inside fronts, with Persian lamb, large storm collar and cuffs of Persian lamb, as cut The Drummer, $55.00.

286. Men's muskrat lined coat, shell of fine English black beaver cloth, with adjustable otter collar, $47.50.

The Kipling.

292. Men's black astrachan coats, 50 inches deep, extra fine selected German-dyed skins, lined with finest quality quilted Italian cloth, chamois pockets and deep roll collar, as cut The Kipling, $45.00.

293. Men's black Corsican lamb coats, large full curl, strong skins, heavy Italian cloth lining and deep storm collar, as cut The Kipling, $20.00.

The Hyde Park.

297. Coachman's bear sett, extra fine natural dark full even fur, including cap, cape and gauntlets, cape with heavy Italian linings, full sweep and high collar, and one-finger gauntlets with lamb linings, as cut The Hyde Park, $75.00.

298. Coachman's bear goat sett, selected full-furred skins, cape with high storm collar, full sweep skirt, lined with durable farmer satin, fur lined one-finger gauntlets, and wedge shape cap, as cut The Hyde Park, $30.00.

Children's Wool Boas.

C.

Children's white wool boas, clean long wool, in the following lengths and prices:

299. 36 inches long, as cut C, 20c.
300. 42   "   "   "   " 25c.
301. 48   "   "   "   " 35c.
302. 54   "   "   "   " 50c.

Hearth Rugs.

303. Grey or white goat plates, clean, soft and well sewn, unlined, size 28 x 66 inches, $2.25.

Fur Robes.

304. Musk-ox robes, extra choice full-furred skins, with heavy plain linings and deep felt border, $50.00.

305. Wolf robes, selected skins, with heavy plush linings and felt edging, $20.00.

306. Black goat robes, best quality, clean soft full-furred skins, with English plush linings and fancy felt border, size 60 x 70 inches, $10.00.

308. Same quality, size 42 x 66 inches, $7.50.

309. Grey goat robes, extra good quality thick full fur, heavy plush lining and two-color felt border size 60 x 70 inches, $6.75.

310. Same quality, size 52 x 66 inches, $5.75.

311. Same quality, size 42 x 66 inches, $4.50.

312. Extra choice white goat robes, very full fur, soft pliable skins, plush lined, size 60 x 70 inches, $7.

313. Same quality, size 52 x 66 inches, $6.00.

314. Same quality, size 42 x 66 inches, $5.00.

Baby Carriage Robes.

"E"

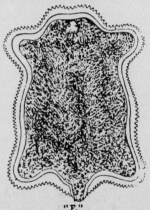

"F."

315. Children's white Thibet carriage robes, the very finest selected skins, long silky curl, with white felt linings, as cut E, $10.00.

316. Children's white Iceland lamb carriage robes, extra choice close curl, with white felt lining and border, as cut E, $5.00.

317. Children's white wool carriage robes, fancy style, with 1 head, 1 tail, and plain white felt linings, as cut F, $3.50.

318. Children's plain white wool carriage robes, size 29 x 33 inches, with white felt linings, as cut E, $2.50.

319. Children's plain white or grey goat carriage robes, thick fur, soft pliable skins, size 33 x 33 inches, lined with plain colored felt, as cut E, $1.50.

The Dawson.

287. Men's prime dark Canadian raccoon coats, 50 inches deep, made from thick full-furred perfectly matched skins and lined with heavy quilted Italian cloth, as cut The Dawson, $47.50.

288. Men's natural dark Canadian raccoon coats, very choice skins, with high collar, chamois pocket and Italian cloth linings, 50 inches deep, as cut The Dawson, $45.00.

289. Men's raccoon coats, very evenly matched, full-furred skins, with quilted farmer satin linings and high storm collar, as cut The Dawson, $40.00.

290. Men's raccoon coats, made from selected dark American skins, with high storm collar, and heavy linings, 50 inches deep, as cut The Dawson, $35.00.

291. Men's dark American raccoon coats, strong well-dressed full-furred skins, with heavy farmer satin lining and deep roll collar, as cut The Dawson, $30.00.

The Skagway.

294. Men's wombat coats, medium dark full-furred skins, with high collar and strong heavy Italian linings, as cut The Skagway, $18.00.

295. Men's wallaby coats, dark even full fur, heavy Italian linings, as cut The Skagway, $17.50.

296. Men's silver wallaby coats, 50 inches deep, with high storm collar and strong heavy linings, as cut The Skagway, $12.50.

Prices of all fur garments subject to fluctuations of the market in raw furs.

LADIES' MEASUREMENT FORM.

1 to 1—Around bust and back under arms.
2 to 2—Around bust and back over arms.
3 to 3—Around waist.
4 to 4—Around hips.
5 to 5—Around neck.
6 to 7—Length of waist.
8 to 9—Centre of back to shoulder.
8 to 10—Centre of back to elbow.
8 to 11—Centre of back to wrist.
12 to 13—Across shoulder.
14 to 15—Armhole.
1 to 16—Across bust, seam to seam.
17 to 18—Length of waist under arms.
Length of garment.

Ladies' Jackets larger than bust 42 will cost more, according to the price of garment.

Dalton Post, about 1890. *Photo by E. J. Glave. University of Alaska Archives.*

Trappers with stretched beaver skins. *Yukon Archives.*

Facing page: A page from the Eaton's Fall & Winter Catalogue, 1899–1900, shows the uses to which Yukon furs were put.

Above, a Tlingit territorial marker on the shore of Atlin Lake (*photo by Julie Cruikshank*). On the facing page, another such marker carved on a tree near Klukshu Flats (*Yukon Archives photo*).

97

A Chilkat hunter in dance costume, about 1900. *Yukon Archives.*

Three white traders: Arthur Harper, Leroy (Jack) McQuesten and Albert Mayo, in 1891, probably at Fortymile. *Courtesy of the Bancroft Library, University of California, Berkeley.*

Fort Selkirk people, photographed about 1898. *Photo by Case & Draper. Alaska Historical Library, Juneau.*

The basic material of this necklace is caribou hide, with indigenous porcupine quill embroidery. The beads were probably traded in from the Pacific coast. The added charms include European buttons and clock springs.

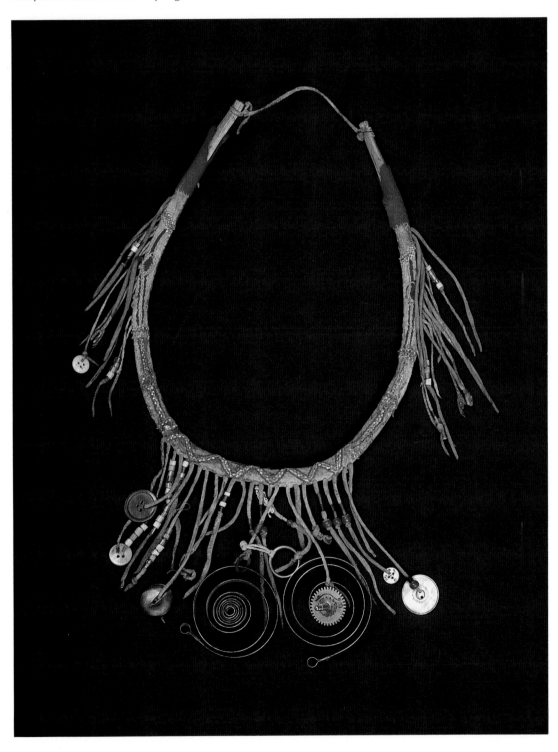

Cultures in Contrast: The Arrival of Strangers 6

ETWEEN 1840 AND 1890, a number of visitors travelled to the part of northwestern North America now known as the Yukon. Fur traders, missionaries, scientists and government officials all had their own reasons for visiting the north. Traders were interested in collecting furs. Missionaries were interested in collecting souls. Scientists wanted to classify and collect facts. Government officials were interested in adding new territories to those they already governed.

Whatever their motives for coming north, most early visitors wrote down their observations. Their journals, letters and reports have been valuable to historians writing about life in the late nineteenth-century Yukon. Frequently, though, the observers' comments tell us more about the cultures of the people *writing* these observations than they tell us about the peoples they were describing. Written records give us many clues about collisions of cultural values in the Yukon during the nineteenth century.

In this chapter we look at how accounts written by traders, missionaries, scientists and government officials reflected cultural values the visitors were bringing with them. Not surprisingly, these accounts are organized differently from the oral accounts of indigenous peoples who observed their arrival. Yet, the written observations of traders, missionaries and others often became the basis on which policy decisions were made – by the Hudson's Bay Company, by the church, and by government. In this way, written documents based on cultural understandings from Europe or from the United Stated often had real economic, political and social consequences for the lives of Yukon people.

Traders and Missionaries:
Victorian Values in the Subarctic

T IS WORTH REVIEWING some points about the fur trade already discussed in Chapter 5, so that we can compare the activities of traders with those of missionaries who came North during the same time period. Between 1840 and 1890, Hudson's Bay Company traders and Church of England missionaries were the main representatives from the outside world in contact with Yukon peoples. On the surface, traders and missionaries were in the North for very different reasons. In practice they often worked together.

Most traders and missionaries came to the Yukon from England and Scotland: a tiny island in western Europe that had virtually exter-

History is culturally ordered, differently so in different societies, according to meaningful schemes of things.
– Marshall Sahlins, *Islands of History*, p vii

Al Wright's *Prelude to Bonanza* makes a major contribution to Yukon history by pulling these written sources together in one book. All the accounts he discusses can be consulted at the Yukon Archives – many of them on microfilm or in fragile documents – and it is valuable to consult them directly. Wright's book weaves together some of the stories those documents tell. He also provides extensive information about the background of their authors.

For an excellent discussion of how Tlingit and Athapaskan people perceived the first Europeans in the Yukon and southwest Alaska, see Catharine McClellan's article "Indian Stories about the First Whites in Northwestern America," available in the Yukon Archives and cited in the bibliography at the end of this book.

Robert Campbell, who established the post at Fort Selkirk, was the son of a sheep farmer from Perthshire, Scotland. *John Bell,* a trader who made the earliest trading excursions into the Peel and Porcupine River country, was a native of the Isle of Mull, off the Scottish coast. *Alexander Murray,* from Argyllshire, became the trader at Fort Yukon. *James Flett,* at La Pierre House, was from the Orkney Islands, off the northern coast of Scotland. Many of these traders were still in, or just beyond, their teens when they began their careers, and as traders they had a startling amount of power for men so young. Campbell was 22; Bell was 19; others were as young as 16. Murray, at 27, was the eldest.

The earliest Church of England missionary in the northern Yukon, *William Kirkby,* was born in Lincolnshire, England. *William Carpenter Bompas,* later Bishop of the Diocese, came from London, as did his missionary wife *Charlotte Selina Bompas.* So did *Vincent Sim,* who went to Rampart House, and *Thomas Canham,* who was based at Fort Selkirk. *Susan Mellett* came to Fortymile from Ireland.

minated its wildlife, depleted its forests and run out of resources by the mid 1800s. The Hudson's Bay Company, with its headquarters in London, recruited many of its northern employees from the Scottish Highlands. During the 1840s, young men who joined the Company and came west and north often did so to escape the ravages of poverty at home. The Highland clearances during the 1830s and 1840s displaced thousands of families who were evicted by landowners planning to establish sheep farms. The disastrous failure of the potato crop in 1846 forced even more Highlanders to emigrate.

The Church Missionary Society, also based in London, sent many of the missionaries who were active in the Yukon after 1860. Most of those men and women came from southern England. They were less likely to be motivated by extreme poverty than by a desire for independence from the restrictions of the Victorian class system.

Traders had little interest in changing the cultures of northern peoples. They realized early on that it was to their advantage to work *with* rather than against ongoing systems of exchange. We have already seen what happened to Robert Campbell when he tried to interfere with longstanding aboriginal trade arrangements.

Once they recognized that it was to their advantage not to interfere with local customs, Hudson's Bay Company traders began to see one of their goals as isolating Native people from any aspect of western culture that might interfere with the overall efficiency of their own trading operations. This often put them at odds with missionaries. From the traders' point of view, missionaries were a distracting force who caused people to cluster around trading posts "for no good reason."

Missionaries, on the other hand, came to the Yukon with a clear assignment to change Native peoples. Their goal was to substitute *their own* beliefs and values for indigenous customs. Christian theology during this period was concerned with fixed meanings – with the idea that there was only one truth, and that good and evil could be clearly defined. Consequently, missionaries were not interested in the spiritual traditions that had always guided the behavior of people living in the Yukon, except when they identified those traditions they wanted to alter. Yukon peoples, on the other hand, were quite open to new ideas and saw no necessary conflict between the idea of accepting the white man's God and retaining their own religious beliefs.

To understand more about the enthusiasm of the earliest missionaries, it is useful to look at events that were taking place in their own countries in the 1850s. England had emerged from the industrial revolution with a strong conviction that it was the social, economic and political centre of the world. Missionaries were swept up by a vision that they had a moral obligation to, as they saw it, "civilize" and "Christianize" peoples throughout the world; in other words, to introduce everyone to the spiritual and cultural values of Victorian Britain.

The business of saving souls was not straightforward, though. Two major mission agencies were in active competition west of the Great Lakes – the Church Missionary Society (CMS), associated with the Church of England, and the Roman Catholic Oblates of Mary

Supplies landing at Fort McPherson in 1892. *Hudson's Bay Company Archives, Provincial Archives of Manitoba.*

"SUBDUE IT AND HAVE DOMINION"

Principles of spirituality in nineteenth-century Christianity and Native American traditions reflect two very different views of society. In the Judeo-Christian tradition, human beings are given a more important role than other creatures and a role *outside of* nature. In fact, the Bible states that at the beginning of time, God told people to "replenish the earth and subdue it: and have dominion over the fish of the sea, and over the fowl of the air, and over every living thing that moveth upon the earth" (Genesis 1:28).

This philosophy was especially popular in Europe during the 1800s. Following the industrial revolution, Man (though never Woman) was seen as capable of conquering nature with the assistance of machines.

By contrast, in Native American traditions, animals and humans share the world. The spirits and power of animals can be sensed in the land, the water, and in all living things. A fundamental principle of such spiritual traditions is that humans must not show arrogant disregard of their environment or everyone will pay a price.

Throughout European history, one can find evidence of a similar tradition. There are poets, scientists and religious devotees who speak of the nonhuman world, and of non-European cultures, with great respect. But in the eighteenth and nineteenth centuries, these voices had little impact on the way most Europeans conducted their affairs. As forests are destroyed, as the ozone layer thins, and as garbage builds up to life-threatening proportions, the principles underlying Native American traditions are now gaining a wider audience.

At Fort McPherson, for example, Rev. Grollier of the OMI was actively working in the community in 1860, but he had to leave because of a brief illness. When he returned in 1861, he was met by one of his former converts who told him, "The minister [*i.e.* Kirkby, representing the Anglican Church] is good to us; he is better than you; he gives us tobacco and tea. He has taken all your pictures and crosses out of the camps." Grollier had to spend that winter living in a tent while Kirkby remained more comfortably as a guest of the Hudson's Bay Company. This is one of many examples of such rivalry cited by Duchaussois in his 1923 volume, *Mid Snow and Ice: The Apostles of the Northwest.*

People who live in Old Crow, Fort McPherson and Fort Yukon speak a language that linguists call Gwich'in, but they sometimes refer to themselves as Loucheux. McDonald used the term Tukudh when he referred to their language.

In 1982, Sarah Simon, wife of the lay preacher in Fort McPherson, James Simon, worked with the Yukon Native Language Centre putting together a booklet of her photographs and recollections entitled *Fort McPherson, N.W.T.: A Pictorial Account of Family, Church, and Community.*

Immaculate (OMI). Even though the Hudson's Bay Company may have been generally hostile to missionaries, in practice the employees of the Company played a critical role in mission activities. Depending on the officer in charge at a post, the Hudson's Bay Company could either make things easier for a missionary by sharing hospitality, or make life very difficult by refusing to grant food, clothing and shelter. In the northern Yukon, the officer in charge at Fort McPherson in the early 1860s had a great deal to do with paving the way for the Anglican CMS and blocking it to the Roman Catholic OMI. Since Fort McPherson was the gateway for European entry to the Yukon in those years, this hospitality had an important effect on church history in the entire territory.

William Kirkby was the first CMS missionary to travel through the Yukon, going from Fort McPherson to Fort Yukon in 1861. He saw the importance of moving quickly to stake out the northwest as Church of England territory. Kirkby recruited two of the more influential early missionaries – Robert McDonald and William Carpenter Bompas. These two men came from very different backgrounds and approached their mission work rather differently.

Immediately after his trip, Kirkby sent word to Robert McDonald, an Anglican priest who had extensive missionary experience on the Red River. Born in that area to an Ojibwa mother and a Scottish trader, McDonald was one of the few CMS missionaries who did not come from England. He agreed to establish a northern mission that would include Fort Yukon, La Pierre House and Fort McPherson. While McDonald shared the Church's enthusiasm for collecting converts, he was less concerned than other missionaries with modifying Gwich'in culture.

McDonald had impressive abilities as a linguist. With the help of his Gwich'in wife, Julia Kutug, he translated the Bible, Anglican prayer book and hymns into the Gwich'in language. He trained lay readers and ministers and established a community-based church that continues to have great significance in the lives of Gwich'in people in the northern Yukon.

McDonald's journals, like those of other missionaries, often refer to the horrifying epidemics of smallpox, whooping cough, tuberculosis and polio that were coming into the area as a result of European trade. Traditionally, spiritual leaders or shamans were expected to cure those who were sick. When they were unable to stop the epidemics, some people hoped that the new missionaries would use the opportunity to demonstrate their own spiritual powers. But aboriginal peoples had never had contact with such diseases and had no immunities to them, and no vaccines existed, so both the traditional healers and the new missionaries were powerless to help.

In 1865, McDonald became ill himself and Kirkby sent a request to London, England, for someone to take over McDonald's duties. William Carpenter Bompas agreed to go. Born to a well-to-do London family, he had originally intended to study law, but changed his mind and was ordained in the Church of England. After working in England for a number of years, he applied to serve overseas, but was turned

Archdeacon McDonald with his son Neil. *Anglican Church of Canada, General Synod Archives.*

Julia Kutug (Mrs Robert McDonald) with her sons Neil and Hugh, and a friend named Mary. *Anglican Church of Canada, General Synod Archives.*

Above, people at the mouth of the Dease River in June 1887. *Photo by George Dawson, National Archives of Canada.* Below, Native students on a hay barge arriving at Chooutla School near Carcross. It was the policy of the school not only to change the students' religion to Christianity, but also to convert them to the agricultural economy favored by most Europeans. As a result, the students learned to cut and bale hay at Ten Mile Ranch, then brought the hay back for use on the school's farm. *Yukon Archives.*

down for work in India and China because his superiors believed he was too old, at thirty, to learn another language. When Kirkby's request for a replacement for McDonald came, Bompas was delighted to comply. By the time he arrived at Fort McPherson, though, he found McDonald recovering, so he decided to expand his missionary efforts south, first at Moosehide on the Yukon River and later at Carcross on the southern lake system.

Bompas's background was very different from McDonald's. Growing up in middle-class, Victorian Britain, Bompas was inevitably influenced by the values of his culture. He was more committed than McDonald to what he saw as "civilizing" and "educating" Native people. Where McDonald was happy to train lay priests and to hold services, Bompas and his wife, Charlotte Selina, undertook to establish schools at various places in the Territory where children could actually live under their instruction and supervision for most of the year. The best-known of these was the Chooutla school at Carcross, which later became the Carcross residential school. It remained open until the late 1960s.

Part of their program reflected an idea, widespread in Britain at the time, that hunters were people whose progress to what Europeans called "civilization" (from the Latin word *civitas* or city) would be hastened if they could be encouraged to give up nomadic lifestyles and made to farm. This idea certainly served the interests of British colonial expansion by justifying the repression of other ways of life in the service of expanding cities like London. It was given further support by the earliest British anthropologists, who described human culture as a kind of pyramid with their own society at the apex and all other societies ranked on an ascending scale from hunting to farming to industrial labour. Church policy took as one of its missions the transformation of hunters to farmers. Despite the dubious wisdom of pursuing agriculture in a subarctic environment, extensive garden patches became part of missions at Moosehide, Carcross and elsewhere. Early photographs from Carcross residential school, for example, show youngsters haying.

Scientists, Mapmakers & Journalists: Classifying the World

IN THE 1870S AND 1880S, visitors with a different perspective began trickling into the territory – naturalists, geologists, and mapmakers eager to chart what they thought of as "unknown territories." Once again, we can see how their approach fits into an established set of values – in this case the western scientific tradition – then centred in Europe and in the eastern United States. By the late nineteenth century, scientists shared a belief that the physical world was an orderly place and that it could be described, analyzed, classified and controlled. Central to their method was their conviction that they could collect "facts" and arrange them into scientifically verifiable categories. In this way, nineteenth-century scientists believed that they

A videotaped production entitled *Old Crow: A Documentary*, was made by Northern Native Broadcasting and aired in 1990. In it, the Anglican priest at Old Crow, Rev. Don Sacks, contrasts the different styles of Archdeacon Robert McDonald and Bishop William Bompas, suggesting that their approaches shaped the Anglican Church differently in different parts of the Yukon. See also *Prelude to Bonanza* and *Part of the Land, Part of the Water* for biographical portraits of McDonald and Bompas.

The Mission School Syndrome, a videotaped documentary produced by Northern Native Broadcasting, traces a history of residential schools in the Yukon. A book entitled *The School at Mopass*, by A. Richard King, gives an account of how the Carcross residential school changed over the years.

Song stick or speaker's staff from the central or southern Yukon, decorated with gull feathers, trade ribbon, and red and black pigment. The figures of caribou are engraved in the forked top of the staff. Below them is a single human figure, connected by a long straight line to the medallion above the handle. The face of the medallion is divided, as if into the red summer world and the white winter world, and the figures in the winter world seem to be travelling in a boat. (Compare Angela Sidney's story, on page 41, in which the animals cross from the winter to the summer world.) *McBride Museum, Whitehorse. Yukon Government photo.*

could make objective sense of the world and contribute to the accumulation of knowledge.

The Far North provided an ideal laboratory for their research. Expeditions were organized. Parties set out with all the enthusiasm of the missionaries and traders who preceded them. Until the 1880s, Tlingit traders still controlled the mountain passes from the Pacific, so the earliest scientists, like the traders and missionaries, entered the territory from the northeast.

If missionaries viewed Native peoples as souls to save, scientists saw them as objects of scientific interest. They frequently classified the aboriginal peoples they encountered as though they were part of the landscape rather than active, thinking human beings. And they often mistakenly saw themselves as separate from and untouched by the natural world, able to manipulate it to their own ends. The outsiders were the observers; the cultural insiders remained the observed.

Older people in Yukon communities, of course, can tell stories *they* heard about some of these early travellers. For example, people on the upper Yukon River had their own classifications for the visitors, calling them *K'och'en*, or "cloud people," because of their pale skins. A number of ancient oral traditions tell of spiritual journeys made by men and women to an unfamiliar world where everything, including people and animals, is white. This white world is a winter world where the characteristics of ordinary reality are reversed so that the traveller must undergo a re-education to understand what he or she is seeing. Some people reasoned that the *K'och'en* were visitors from this world. They observed carefully and from a distance as the white "cloud people" passed by in their boats. Many early reports from the upper Yukon River include sentences like "Once again, we saw no Indians." It is clear from oral histories, though, that indigenous people certainly saw the strangers.

Robert Kennicott, a 25-year-old naturalist with the Smithsonian Institution in Washington, spent the winter of 1860–61 conducting plant and animal studies at Fort McPherson and much of the following winter at La Pierre House. He was immensely popular with the traders there and so inspired them with his interest in collecting that for years after his departure they continued to send "collections" to his museum.

An ambitious plan to lay a telegraph line from Oregon north through the Yukon and Alaska to Siberia caught Kennicott's attention because he saw the possibilities it held for doing scientific research. He accepted a position as Director of the Scientific Corps with the Overland Telegraph Company. Unfortunately, the stresses involved in putting together the expedition were overwhelming, and Kennicott died of a heart attack in Alaska in 1865. Kennicott's work was taken over by another young scientist from the Smithsonian, William Dall, who was 21 years old at the time. Dall spent his time on the lower Yukon River, in what is now Alaska, and reported what he learned from the Native peoples on that part of the river. He never actually visited the upper Yukon River, but he nevertheless published his classification of upriver languages. He identified the upper Yukon River languages by names that are still used today: "Vunta Kutchin" on the Porcupine, the "Han

On the other side of the medallion are the figures of two more caribou. *Yukon Government photo.*

For more information about Kennicott, Dall and the Overland Telegraph Company, see *Prelude to Bonanza.*

Linguists are still puzzled by some of
Dall's terms because it's not quite clear
how they were used. Tutchone, for
example, is now the official name of the
language spoken in the central Yukon,
but it is not a term that elders used until
recently.

Kutchin" on the river above Fort Yukon, and the "Tutchone Kutchin"
further up the Yukon River.

One major expedition from this period that did not include scientists was led by Frederick Schwatka, a lieutenant with the US Army. By the late 1880s, the Tlingits were losing control of the mountain passes and Schwatka's was one of the earliest parties to enter the Yukon from the southwest. His assignment was to make a map of the upper Yukon River, describing the geography and noting the locations of Native peoples.

Schwatka handled the notion of classification rather differently from scientists. His method of recording names of lakes, rivers and mountains set off a debate that continues today. He chose to ignore the Native names he heard for topographic features, dismissing them as "difficult to pronounce," and replaced them with names of his patrons or of scientists he admired. We have already seen that indigenous place names link people and their stories to place. English place names are more often graffiti, saying "I was here." Schwatka went a step further, naming places for people who had never even visited the Yukon. He named Lindeman Lake and Haeckel Hill for German academics, Watson River and Marsh Lake for American scientists, Nordenskiold River and Nares Lake for Swedish and British explorers, and Wheaton River and Michie Mountain for American military officers. Schwatka published detailed drawings of some of the places he visited, but his written reports contain many inaccuracies and drew harsh criticism from later travellers who tried to follow his maps.

See Dawson's *Report on an Exploration*,
p 17.

Schwatka's most vocal critic was a geologist, George Dawson. In 1887 a geological expedition headed by Dawson, with geologist R. G. McConnell and surveyor William Ogilvie, made a more systematic inventory of the same area. Each of these men explored a different part of the Yukon. Their surveys produced the first really thorough studies of Yukon geology and each later published an account of his journey.

Dawson was particularly energetic, even though he had been partially crippled by a childhood disease. Unlike Schwatka, Dawson took pains to record what Native people told him about their activities, their languages, and their environment. His report includes detailed sections on plants, animals and rocks. He also recorded lists of place names and names for plants and animals in Native Yukon languages.

He was thoughtful enough to notice that the local trails were quite different from those followed by the Europeans: Europeans followed waterways, especially the Yukon River, because they travelled by boat. Referring to Native travellers, Dawson noted in 1887 that "most of their travelled routes appear, indeed, to run nearly *at right angles to the drainage*," and that people tended to use rafts to cross rivers and then left them behind. This calls into question some of the observations whites had made about the location of aboriginal settlements. The Yukon River was an axis for European explorers, but the original peoples made much more comprehensive use of the land. They came to the Yukon River in salmon season, but much of the rest of their year was spent hunting game and fishing in lakes some distance from rivers.

George Mercer Dawson. *Photo by William Notman & Son, Montreal. Yukon Archives.*

George Dawson was born in Pictou, Nova Scotia in 1849. A gifted scholar, he studied geology in Edinburgh and London, and then returned to Canada where he carried out research on the Queen Charlotte Islands, the Skeena and Peace Rivers, the Assiniboine, and in Alberta. He was made Assistant Director of the Geological Survey of Canada in 1883 and undertook the Yukon expedition in 1887. His part in the expedition involved surveying the Stikine River to the Dease River, then following Robert Campbell's route to Fort Selkirk and returning to the coast via the Chilkoot.

William Ogilvie, born in Ottawa in 1846, began working as a Dominion Land Surveyor in 1869. By the time he joined Dawson's expedition, he had already helped survey the Saskatchewan-Alberta border. His northern assignment was to determine the exact location of the Canada-Alaska boundary. When the United States purchased Alaska from Russia in 1867, they inherited the Russian position on the boundary, originally defined in the 1825 Anglo-Russian agreement. Because the area had never been surveyed, and because there were real disputes about where it actually *was,* the location of parts of that boundary remained in question until the end of the century. Ogilvie's contribution to this expedition was to survey the Chilkoot Pass to the head of the Yukon River, then down that river to establish as closely as possible the location of the 141st meridian, separating Canada and the United States. Ogilvie later became the first Commissioner of the Yukon.

Richard McConnell, born in 1857 at Chatham, Québec, began working for the Geological Survey of Canada in 1879. He and Dawson both travelled up the Stikine River to reach the Yukon, separating at the Dease River. From there, McConnell travelled north and east, recording his observations about the eastern Yukon and Mackenzie Valley.

Books written by Dawson, Ogilvie, and McConnell are all available at the Yukon Archives and are listed in the bibliography at the end of this book.

Placer gold is gold in the form of sediments or particles on the earth's surface. The relative ease of obtaining such gold made it attractive to prospectors who found it in many rivers on the west coast of North America.

Again we learn about the changes by comparing oral and written documents. When the German geographer, Aurel Krause, arrived in southwestern Alaska in 1883, he heard from coastal Tlingit people that the preferred route to the Yukon River had once been via Kusawa Lake. By the 1880s this route was no longer being used. Mrs Annie Ned, an elder who spent the early part of her married life on Kusawa Lake, points out that Kusawa Lake got its Tlingit name because it was on this early trade route, and that Tlingits called it *Koosawu Àa*, "long lake," because it took such a long time to travel its length into the interior.

As geologists, Dawson and McConnell had additional interests – identifying mineral resources. More and more people were becoming convinced that the northern Cordillera contained placer gold deposits similar to those of California and British Columbia. Dawson actually predicted in 1887 that a major discovery was inevitable (and was later rewarded when Dawson City was named after him). For all Dawson's sensitive descriptions of indigenous peoples, he, too, saw them as quite peripheral to the new historical trends in the North.

One final expedition at the close of this period, in 1890, deserves mention because it provides one of the most descriptive accounts of aboriginal life in the Yukon prior to the gold rush – in writing, in sketches and in photographs. Edward J. Glave, whom we have already met, was the journalist, artist and photographer accompanying the Frank Leslie Exploring Expedition. A seasoned traveller, he came to the Yukon from Africa where he had been a member of the Stanley expedition (and died in Africa on another expedition a few years later). Glave's written accounts provide one of the few detailed descriptions of daily lives of Southern Tutchone speakers who were living some distance from the Yukon River.

Written accounts from this period, then, give us an interesting snapshot of what late nineteenth-century visitors *did* see, but what about the things they missed? Two major shortcomings confront us when we try to learn about the history of Yukon First Nations from written documents.

First, we should remember that the Yukon was a dynamic and changing place by the time the first visitors arrived and began writing down their observations. In many cases, visitors who were writing in the late 1800s were documenting the consequences of European intrusion rather than features of aboriginal lifestyle. By the 1880s the Tlingit and Athapaskan fur trade was tapering off; it probably had its heyday between 1840 and 1870. By 1890, many coastal Tlingit people were working in canneries and independent white traders were providing inlanders with alternative places to trade their furs.

Secondly, most early reports from the southern Yukon provide observations from a narrow corridor along the Yukon River. A sharp contrast occurs when we listen to oral tradition. When elders talk about early centres of population in the southern Yukon, they always refer to Hutshi and Aishihik. When we turn to the written record, these places are rarely named because they were some distance from the Yukon River, far from the routes used by most white visitors. When Chief Jim Boss made the first Yukon land claim from Lake Laberge in 1902, he gave population figures for southern communities. He was trying to show how *small* the numbers were in order to demonstrate how seriously his people had been affected by white man's diseases. Even so, the figures he gives for Aishihik and Hutshi are considerably larger than for other communities.

E. J. Glave

Throughout my letter I have retained the native names of geographical points wherever I could learn them. In my opinion, this should always be studied. The Indian names of the mountains, lakes and rivers are natural land marks for the traveller, whoever he may be; to destroy these by substituting words of a foreign tongue is to destroy the natural guides. You ask for some point and mention its native name; your Indian guide will take you there. Ask for the same place in your substituted English and you will not be understood. Travelling in Alaska [sic] has already sufficient difficulties, and they should not be increased by changing all the picturesque Indian names. Another very good reason why these names should be preserved is that some tradition of tribal importance is always connected with them. These people have no written language, but the retention of their native names is an excellent medium through which to learn their history.

E. J. Glave took a very different view from Frederick Schwatka on the subject of place names. Glave wrote these words in 1890.

PEOPLE THE VISITORS DIDN'T SEE

Chief Jim Boss, from Lake Laberge, attempted to file the first claim to ancestral lands by Yukon First Nations in 1902.

At his request, a letter was sent to Ottawa by a local lawyer, T. W. Jackson. The document outlines Jim Boss's concern that newcomers were taking possession of hunting grounds, and that the people were dying as a result of new diseases. He lists communities in order to show how their numbers had shrunk during the years just prior to 1902. Numbers are startlingly lower near the Yukon River than in more distant communities like Hutshi and Aishihik:

Names listed in claim	Population	Probable locations
Marsh Lake	15	McClintock River
Tagish	30	Tagish
Hoochi	200	Hutshi
Kluchoo	25	Kloo Lake
Iseaq	250	Aishihik
Klukshoo	80	Klukshu
Gaysuchu	50	Big Salmon (Gyò Cho Chú)
Tatsuchu	15	Carmacks (?)
Kloosulchuk	35	Minto
Haseena	90	Ross River

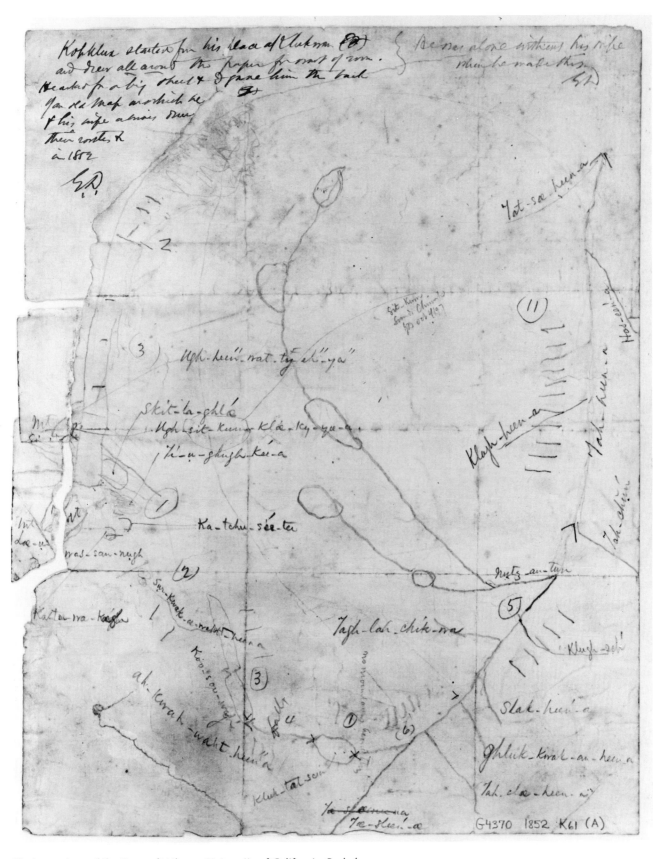

Photo courtesy of the Bancroft Library, University of California, Berkeley.

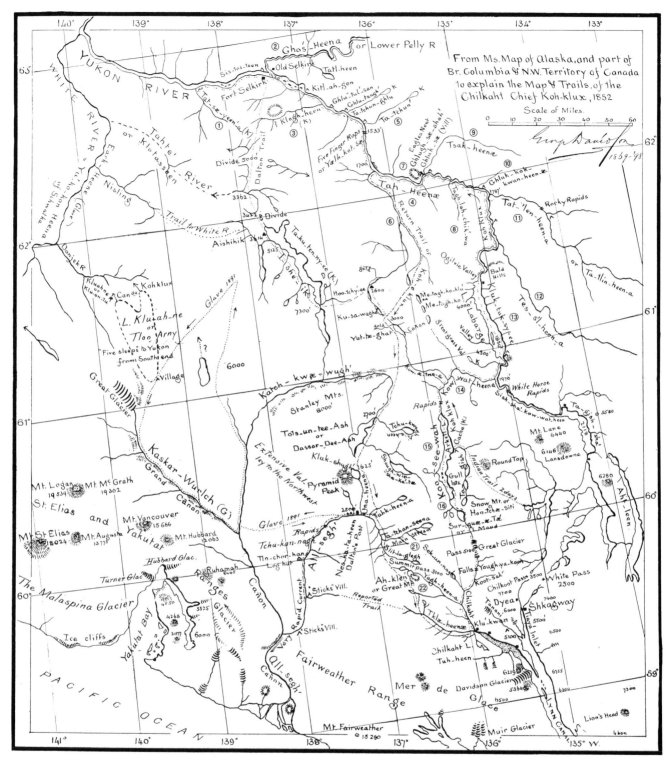

The following labels appear on the map:

From Ms. Map of Alaska, and part of
Br. Columbia & N.W. Territory of Canada
to explain the Map & Trails of the
Chilkaht Chief Koh-klux, 1852
Scale of Miles.

George Davidson
1869-98

Facing page: The Kohklux Map. This rare document allows us to see the combined perspectives of indigenous knowledge and scientific tradition.

For generations, Athapaskan and Tlingit people in the Yukon drew maps, on the ground or in words. The map shown here was drawn in 1869 by a Chilkat Chief whose name is recorded as "Kohklux." He lived in Klukwan, Alaska, but had travelled inland to the Yukon River with trading parties, and as a young man he led the party that destroyed Fort Selkirk in 1852. His map had a particular purpose: to show foot trails between the Pacific coast and the trading post at Fort Selkirk, on the Yukon River. He also pinpointed camps, caches and settlements along the route.

[continued on page 117]

Law and Order: Extending the Empire

BY THE 1870S AND 1880S, prospectors were arriving on the upper Yukon River, many of them bringing experience from the goldfields of California and British Columbia. As more outsiders arrived, the question of who actually "owned" the territory arose. It is very clear from written documents that this question was only discussed as an issue of ownership between Canada and the United States. At no time did those two governments consider that First Nations might have any stake in that ownership. The United States had purchased Alaska from Russia in 1867. They had agreed that the 141st meridian would be the boundary line with Canada. Ogilvie's survey gave a physical location to that line in 1887. Nevertheless, the majority of prospectors by this time were American and many of them were reluctant to be ruled by Canadian law.

In 1894, the Government of Canada sent out its own "fact finding mission" under the direction of Inspector Charles Constantine, largely to demonstrate their claim to the area. Born in England in 1849, the son of an Anglican clergyman, Constantine had already been working with the Northwest Mounted Police for some years. Armed with reports by Frederick Schwatka and George Dawson, he set out from the Lynn Canal over the Chilkoot Pass, making his way down the Yukon River to Fortymile.

Constantine's comments from this expedition show that his main concern was for the prospectors. He made very few references to Native peoples, and when he did, they were unsympathetic. Even more than before, Native people appear in written records as "background" to a different drama being staged by newcomers. By now, some of the missionaries were taking more active roles in trying to defend the rights of Native people. Bishop Bompas, for example, organized a meeting of Han people with Constantine, at which the bishop acted as interpreter. The Han delegation complained that white miners were shooting their dogs. Constantine responded by defending the miners and telling the hunters to tie up their dogs.

A far more tragic misunderstanding of concepts of justice occurred four years later in 1898. Four Tagish men were charged with murder when a prospector was shot near Marsh Lake. They were taken to Dawson City, tried in court and three of them were sentenced to death. A comparison of oral and written accounts suggests that the circumstances involved conflicting understandings of "law."

Just as missionaries originally displayed little interest in the religious systems of Native people, so lawmakers showed no interest in their legal systems. If either Constantine or the judge involved in the trial of the Tagish men had asked people from the upper Yukon River how disputes were normally settled, he might have learned that there were clear rules for handling conflict. If, for example, someone from the Crow moiety harmed a person from the Wolf side, all Crow people would have been responsible for arranging compensation. The terms of that compensation would be negotiated between the two sides but the offender's side was responsible for starting the discussions. Because

Oral accounts about the incident and written transcripts from the trial are compared in the paper "Oral Traditions and Written Accounts: An Incident from the Klondike Gold Rush" by Julie Cruikshank.

such questions were not asked, and because of assumptions about Native peoples made by newcomers, First Nations were forcibly subjected to Canadian laws, and customary ways of managing conflict were marginalized.

Written Documents and Yukon Lifestyles in the Late Nineteenth Century

THIS CHAPTER only skims the surface of written records available in the Yukon Archives. We can see, though, that these records, like any accounts, present a partial picture. Visitors collected furs, souls, facts and land, and they left a detailed, if somewhat limited, record of their experiences. They did not ask questions about indigenous systems of religion, knowledge and law because they didn't consider those questions significant. This is not because the visitors were willfuly distorting what they wrote. They were simply operating, as we all do, from a particular historical context, from deep-seated cultural values.

What the documents suggest is that written records, like oral accounts, have to be used very carefully if we are trying to use them to understand something about the past. The limitations of the written record make it particularly important to record additional oral accounts from elders who may have heard about these times and may be able to tell us how events were understood by cultural insiders. The next chapter discusses one such example: the "discovery" of gold on the Klondike River.

[continued from page 115]
Kohklux drew his map for a visiting scientist named George Davidson, who added the place names from Kohklux's dictation. According to Davidson, "at his own suggestion, Kohklux proposed to draw upon paper his route to and from Selkirk." Kohklux then drew two maps, one alone and one in consultation with his wives. Davidson's notes at the top of the map on page 114 tell us that this is the one drawn by Kohklux alone.

Some years later, Davidson had the Kohklux Map redrawn to fit the rules of modern map making. The redrawn map, which Davidson published in 1901, is reproduced on page 115. We have added numbers to this map to make it easier to compare it with the original, drawn by Kohklux. (Note that these numbers *do not* correspond to the numbers which Davidson pencilled on the Kohklux Map itself.)

North is not a fixed direction on the Kohklux Map, so to keep North at the top, the map must be turned as it is read.

In the following list, the *numbers* are those we have added to the redrawn map, but the *italicized names* come from the Kohklux Map itself. Starting at the upper right, and moving clockwise, the following names can be read on the Kohklux Map:

1 *Tat-sae-heen-a* [Hayes Creek & lower Selwyn River];
2 *Hos-een-a* [Pelly River];
3 *Klagh-heen-a* [Big Creek];
4 *Tah-heen-a* [Yukon River between Laberge and Five Finger Rapids];
5 *Tah-chun* [Tatchun River];
6 *Nutz-an-tun* [Nordenskiold River];
7 *Klugh-seh* [Eagles Nest Bluff];
8 *Tagh-lah-chik-wa* [Claire Creek];
9 *Shak-heen-a* [Little Salmon River];

10 *Ghluk-kwak-an-heen-a* [Walsh Creek];
11 *Tah-clae-heen-a* [Big Salmon River];
12 *Tae-sleen-a* [Teslin River];
13 *Kluk-tat-sein* [Lake Laberge];
14 *[Ah-]kwah-waht-heena* [Takhini River];
15 *Koo-sou-wagh* [Kusawa Lake];
16 *Sur-kwak-a-waht-heen-a* [Kusawa River];
17 *Ka-tu-wa-kaegh* [possibly the Primrose Valley];
18 *Ka-tchu-see-ta* [unidentified];
19 *Ti-u-ghugh-kae-a* [unidentified];
20 *Ugh-sit-kum-klae-ky-yee-a* [unidentified];
21 *Skit-la-ghlae* [Upper Tatshenshini River];
22 *Ugh-heen-nat-ty-eh-ya* [Kelsall River].

On the redrawn map, a few of these names are omitted and several are spelled differently.

A group of people identified as ''David's Band,'' camped near Fortymile, in the 1890s. On the opposite page is a man identified as ''Indian Henry,'' a member of the band. *Courtesy of the Bancroft Library, University of California, Berkeley.*

Keish (Skookum Jim) and his family.
From left to right, the figures are:
1 unidentified; **2** Keish's brother-in-law,
George Carmack; **3** Keish's wife,
Daaku̱xda.éit'; **4** their daughter
Saayna.aat (Daisy); **5** Keish himself;
6 Kooɬseen (Patsy Henderson). *Yukon
Archives.*

Skookum Jim or Keish: Another View of the Klondike Gold Rush

7

EVENTS surrounding successive gold rushes in California, British Columbia, the Yukon and Alaska, during the mid and late nineteenth century, continue to exert a peculiar fascination for many audiences. This is particularly true of the Klondike rush, perhaps because its circumstances draw together so many elements essential to European and American folklore. A singular glamor is associated with gold in any period of history, but its discovery in the Yukon in 1896 coincided with a world depression and gave hope to thousands of unemployed men and women. It was called a "poor man's gold rush," because individual prospectors could go to the Yukon with relatively little capital, egged on by dreams of fortunes waiting to be found in the creek beds and gravel bars. All that seemed to be required was a willingness to take the risks involved in travelling to the extreme northwest corner of North America.

In hindsight, of course, we know that the Klondike gold rush was part of a much larger, less glamorous process – the expansion of the new Canadian state into what was seen as the margins. Very few goldseekers even found claims to stake after they had completed the strenuous trip over the Coast Mountains and down the Yukon River. The most permanent effect of the gold rush was the establishment of a framework for administration of the Territory from Ottawa, the new nation's capital. Institutions dating from this time continue to have far-reaching implications for everyone living in the Yukon.

This gold rush has produced an enormous literature, but in thousands of written pages we find very few references to indigenous peoples who watched the changes come and were affected by them. Between 1896 and 1900, tens of thousands of would-be prospectors and miners converged on one small area of the Klondike River. The vast majority came by the same route, climbing the Chilkoot Pass and then travelling down the Yukon River to Dawson City. We are left to imagine the impact of this torrent of visitors on aboriginal peoples living along the route and at the site of Dawson City itself, because so few travellers even mentioned Native peoples in their journals.

Stories passed on by word of mouth, describing the gold rush from the perspective of indigenous peoples, may some day become a significant part of the written record. This chapter examines one particular incident in order to show some of the possibilities that exist for combining written and oral accounts. Comparing such accounts shows

Kate Carmack tells me all that. They just go look for her. They're not looking for gold!
– Mrs Kitty Smith

When Skookum Jim found gold, that's the time everything changed. This time we can't do it now, can't travel around. People just stay where they stay.
– Mrs Annie Ned

how ideas about family and community organization – which differ from one culture to another – may influence the *interpretation* of events.

One reference to Native people does turn up repeatedly in written accounts of the Klondike gold rush. The issue of how the initial "discovery" of gold was made has been controversial, partly because of the circumstances surrounding the claim. The knowledge that gold existed was hardly new. For years, there had been lively discussion among prospectors about the likelihood of a major gold strike in the area. Robert Campbell had made reference to gold near Fort Selkirk in his journals as early as 1850. Missionaries like Robert McDonald noted traces of gold in Birch Creek near the Yukon-Alaska border in the 1870s. Geologist George Dawson predicted a major find when he made his survey in the late 1880s. Yet the term "discovery" always refers to the same event – the almost accidental location of a creek where placer gold lay in amounts sufficient to signal the major rush.

This event is still celebrated annually on 17 August, when a Territory-wide holiday, Discovery Day, is observed and festivities are organized in Dawson City.

Names of individuals associated with this event appear repeatedly in accounts of the gold rush: Skookum Jim, his sister Kate, Dawson Charlie (all Tagish Natives) and Kate's non-Native husband George Carmack. The stories about Skookum Jim that appear in the *written* record represent him as a kind of frontier folk hero, the archetypal self-made man. His activities are often described and interpreted symbolically in these accounts, as evidence that even the most improbable individual can find riches and thereby transform his own life and the society around him.

Oral accounts from his own community, though, describe him from a very different perspective and give us a rare opportunity to compare accounts passed on in the gold rush literature with those passed on by individuals who knew the principal actors personally. A comparison of written and oral accounts shows the significance of cultural context in bringing the lens of interpretation to "facts."

The Written Record

SKOOKUM JIM's name appears early in historical records. William Ogilvie, whose work as a government surveyor was discussed in Chapter 6, employed him as a packer in 1887 to carry supplies over the Chilkoot Pass. He marvelled at the heavy loads Jim carried, noting that this was the reason "Skookum" (meaning "strong" in Chinook jargon) had become part of his English name.

Chinook jargon, from which the term "Skookum" comes, was a pidgin language containing elements from various Northwest Coast languages and from English and French. It was used as a trade language on the coast.

The best-known written account of Skookum Jim's adventures describes his association with the white prospector George Carmack, who was the husband of Jim's sister Kate. In 1896, Jim, Kate, her husband George, and Jim's and Kate's sister's son, Charlie, travelled down the Yukon River allegedly prospecting for gold. Pierre Berton, whose popular book about the Klondike gold rush is probably the most widely read account of the period, paints a rather one-dimensional picture of Jim. Berton's portrayal is ethnocentric, like the written accounts on which it is based, but it makes Jim understandable – and attractive – to readers of gold rush folklore:

Two people from the Peel River country, about 1900. The older is one of the "Dawson Boys" – men from the Peel River who traded in Dawson during the gold rush. *Yukon Archives.*

One of the few early writers who gave a detailed account of his experiences with Yukon Natives was Tappan Adney, a journalist who spent the winter of 1901 with Han people not far from Dawson City. He wrote a book, *The Klondike Stampede,* and two articles about his experiences hunting with families on the upper Klondike River.

Richard Slobodin, an anthropologist who lived in Fort McPherson during the winters of 1938–9 and 1946–7, interviewed a number of Gwich'in men who had travelled to the Klondike during the height of the rush. These men later became known as "the Dawson Boys" in their own community. After experiencing the heady life in Dawson at the turn of the century – the dance halls, gambling and bars – the Dawson Boys returned to become a conservative force in their community, the strongest advocates of retaining community traditions.

For further reading, see Adney's and Slobodin's accounts, cited at the end of this book.

See Berton, *Klondike*, pp 42–43.

[He was] a giant of a man, supremely handsome with his high cheek bones, his eagle's nose, and his fiery black eyes – straight as a gun barrel, powerfully built and known as the best hunter and trapper on the river. . . . Just as Carmack wished to be an Indian, Jim longed to be a white man – in other words, a prospector. He differed from the others in his tribe in that he displayed the white man's kind of ambition.

Near the Klondike River, they met another prospector, Robert Henderson, who advised Carmack that he knew a good place to look for gold. Henderson was willing to share the information with Carmack, but not with his Native friends. Jim, Charlie, George and Kate therefore went on their way, and when they accidentally found gold a few days later, very close to the place Henderson had identified, they neglected to go back and tell him. So rapid was the staking rush following their discovery that Henderson missed out and became the tragic figure of the drama, defeated by his own arrogance.

Jim, George, Kate and Charlie travelled briefly to Seattle with their newfound wealth. By then, according to reports Carmack filed with the government, their gold production had exceeded $200,000. They set out to spend it, Klondike style. Seattle newspapers gleefully reported on their high-rolling life, including stories that may have been untrue about Kate blazing her way up a wooden stairway to her hotel room with a hatchet. But the romance and the glamor were short-lived.

Carmack abandoned Kate, leaving her penniless and severing his ties with his brother-in-law, Skookum Jim. He married a white woman, Marguerite Saftig, who had formerly run a cigar store in Dawson City. Charlie drowned in 1909, after falling from the Carcross bridge. Jim continued prospecting, making lengthy trips along the Teslin, Pelly, McMillan, Stewart and Upper Liard Rivers, but he failed to make another major strike and his health began to deteriorate. He died in 1916.

The Oral Accounts

MANY YUKON ELDERS living in the southern Yukon knew Skookum Jim personally. During the 1980s Mrs Angela Sidney, Mrs Kitty Smith and Mrs Annie Ned each recorded her life story, and each made reference to Skookum Jim in her account.

Mrs Sidney's father's mother and Skookum Jim's mother were sisters, making the two men brothers by the Tagish system of kinship reckoning. Consequently Skookum Jim was Angela Sidney's uncle. She knew him from the time she was a child until his death in 1916 and helped to nurse him during his final illness.

Mrs Smith married Skookum Jim's sister's son, Billy Smith. After marriage, she also developed a close friendship with her husband's aunt, Kate Carmack, and heard her gold rush stories many times.

Mrs Ned says that her family and Skookum Jim's family once began discussions about a possible marriage between the two of them.

Skookum Jim's lawyer, W.L. Phelps, kept detailed notes and copies of correspondence between himself, Jim, Jim's daughter Daisy, and Daisy's guardian Percy R. Peele. Much of the correspondence deals with Jim's will; however, it also documents changes that were occurring in Jim's and Daisy's lives. Copies of the papers and letters are part of the Yukon Archives manuscript collection.

STAKING THE CLAIM

Writing his account of the Klondike gold rush in 1913, William Ogilvie reported:

When I first entered the country in 1887, I found [Carmack] at Dyea Pass. . . . I employed him to help me over the pass and through his influence got a good deal of assistance from his Indian friends. Skookum Jim and Tagish Charlie were both there and packed for me. Skookum well earned his sobriquet of "Skookum" or "strong" for he carried one hundred and fifty-six (156) pounds of bacon over the pass for me at a single trip. This might be considered a heavy load anywhere on any roads, but over the stony moraine of a glacier, as the first half of the distance is, and then up a steep pass, climbing more than three thousand feet in six or seven miles, some of it so steep that the hands have to be used to assist one up, certainly is a stiff test of strength and endurance.

Before publishing his account, Ogilvie went back to interview the participants again about the actual events surrounding the discovery and staking of the claim. He reports his conversation with Skookum Jim:

After satisfying themselves that they had the best spot and deciding to stake and record there, [Jim, Charlie and Carmack] got into a dispute as to who should stake discovery claim, Jim claiming it by right of discovery and Carmac[k] claiming it, Jim says, on the ground that an Indian would not be allowed to record it. Jim says the difficulty was finally settled by agreeing that Carmac[k] was to stake and record the discovery claim, and assign half of it, or a half interest in it, to Jim, so on the morning of August 17th, 1896, Carmac[k] staked discovery claim five hundred feet in length up and down the direction of the creek valley, and N° 1 below discovery of the same length; both the full width of the valley bottom, and from base to base of the hill on either side, as the regulations then read. N° 2 below was staked for Tagish Charlie, and N° 1 above for Skookum Jim.

A community organization now based in Whitehorse, the Skookum Jim Friendship Centre, undertook an oral history project in 1975, interviewing a number of elders from the southern Yukon about their memories of Skookum Jim. These tapes, and transcripts of the interviews, "The Skookum Jim Oral History Project," can be consulted at the Yukon Archives.

For the life stories of Mrs Sidney, Mrs Smith and Mrs Ned, see *Life Lived Like a Story: Life Stories of Three Yukon Native Elders*.

Keish (Skookum Jim), with his wife
Daaku̠x̠da.éit', and their daughter
Saayna.aat. *Yukon Archives.*

After some negotiations, her family decided that Skookum Jim's life had been changed too dramatically by the events of the gold rush and arranged for her to marry someone else. In the course of the discussions, though, she heard first-hand accounts about the events of the "discovery."

Skookum Jim's real name was *Keish*. Jim's mother was a Tagish woman who had married a Tlingit man; the Tlingit name Keish belonged to her Dakl'aweidí clan but affirmed her husband's ancestry. At the time of Keish's birth, sometime after the mid-1800s, Tlingit economic influence in the interior was probably at its height. We have already noted that whenever possible, Tlingits formalized trading partnerships with their interior neighbors through ties of marriage. The interior Tagish people formally adopted Tlingit clans, clan names, personal names, traditions and even Tlingit language as these marriages became common. Keish was born of such a union.

When Mrs Sidney talks about Skookum Jim, she draws attention not to his exceptional physical strength but rather to how well he understood the social obligations that were part of his world. She begins by talking about how he came to have Frog as his spirit helper. She goes on to talk about his encounter with Tl'anaxéedakw or "Wealth Woman." She explains how Keish behaved as any Tagish man should, by taking responsibility for the safety of his sisters. She interprets his behaviour from the perspective of the events described in the following stories, rather than from any desire to be a prospector or to discover gold.

As a young man, Keish once saved the life of a frog trapped in a deep hole. Later the same frog returned to him on two different occasions, once in its animal form when it healed a wound he had received, and once again in the form of a woman, showing him a gold-tipped walking cane which would direct him toward his fortune downriver. People credit Keish's Frog helper with a significant role in his eventual discovery of gold.

His encounter with Tl'anaxéedakw was equally significant. A complex figure in Tagish mythology, she richly rewards anyone who hears her, catches her and follows a particular ritual that everyone who knows the story would remember. Both Jim and Charlie heard her, but run as they might, they were unable to overtake her, says Mrs Sidney. Consequently, the money which came their way after the discovery of gold did not last.

While superhuman beings may have helped Tagish people to explain the actual discovery of gold, Mrs Sidney, Mrs Smith and Mrs Ned also emphasize Keish's understanding of his social responsibilities when they talk about his life. Information provided by Mrs Sidney when she was preparing her family history makes this clearer. A number of individuals appear in this story, and it is easier to follow the details if you refer to her family tree.

Skookum Jim's father, Kaachgaawáa, was the local head of the Deisheetan clan. Keish's mother, Gus'duteen, belonged to the Dakl'aweidí clan. Kaachgaawáa made his headquarters at the place where Bennett Lake flows into Nares Lake, at the site of the present village of

Catharine McClellan has compared eight accounts of the Frog Helper story and numerous references to Wealth Woman in her article, "Wealth Woman and Frogs among the Tagish Indians," cited in the bibliography. This article is available in the Yukon Archives pamphlet collection.

Angela Sidney

When people go to Skagway,
they always camp at that little lake back of the section house at
      Bennett [on the White Pass railway].
It's too little to have a name, that lake.

They were camping there on the lakeside when they heard that baby
      crying –
Skookum Jim heard it – then Dawson Charlie heard it.
Here they got up to go after it.
Patsy [Henderson] went with them – he went a little way, but he got
      scared, started crying – he was still a kid yet.

"Crazy me," he tells us later.
"That's why I never get rich."

And they tried to chase it around – around the lake.
It kept disappearing.
That's why their money didn't last after they found gold.
They found money alright, but it didn't last.

The night was pitch dark.
You know September, how dark it gets at nights?
And you know how bushy that place is!

Grandma Hammond, *Aandaax'w,* said she heard that baby too.
She heard it, but she never tried.
She thought it was her sister coming, and here, no! – nobody showed
      up.
So when it quit, she started to cry – she told us herself.
That's around Bennett.
But she used to make money like everything, sewing you know.

My mother said they went to Ptarmigan Mountain, back of Tagish.
K'asmbáa Dzéłe', in Tagish Language; *X'eis'awaa Shaayí* in Tlingit.

In the evening they went to bed.
Fire started to go down a little bit.
They didn't have tent or anything – it was just open.
They got a fly tent, though.
They dried some meat.
All of a sudden, at night time, baby started to cry.
"Waa, Waa, Waa," and they hear that mother making a noise.
They got up, sat up, told each other,
"You hear that noise?"
My brother Johnny heard it.

That's why he's lucky all the time.

Carcross. He and his wife had a large family. Eight of their children, two brothers and six sisters, survived to adulthood and were living in the 1890s.

By the late 1880s pressure from prospectors and traders was breaking down the Tlingit trade monopoly. Marriages between coastal and interior people continued to be important, though, and Keish and his brother both married coastal Tlingit women during the time they worked as packers for prospectors entering the Yukon. But sometime early in the 1890s, the elder brother, Tlákwshaan, died in one of the influenza epidemics sweeping the coast.

Three of Keish's sisters also married coastal men, but in each case illness and death intervened. His eldest sister fell victim to influenza and died shortly after her marriage. Because marriages were contracts establishing important alliances between kin groups, rather than just between individuals, her husband's clan requested that one of her sisters be sent to replace her, as was the custom. Another daughter, Aagé, travelled down to the coast to become the second wife.

But even before this marriage could take place, the husband fell ill and died. Because the deceased man had no unmarried brother, custom dictated that his sister's son, who was of the same clan, should become Aagé's new husband. Aagé and her husband had a daughter, but a few years later and just before the birth of their second child, the husband was killed in a fight about which clan had the right to pack prospectors' goods over the pass. The young widow requested that she be allowed to return to her own family, and her husband's family agreed, but only on the condition that she leave her eldest child with them to raise. Carcross elders remember this child by the English name Susie George. The marriage, the deaths, and the loss of her first child had taken a toll, and for a variety of reasons, Aagé asked her mother to look after her other child, Louise, while she left with a prospector known as Mr Wilson. In this way, Aagé became the first of Skookum Jim's sisters to go downriver with a white prospector.

A third sister, known as Kate or Shaaw Tláa, also married a coastal Tlingit man, her mother's brother's son, in a conventional alliance. They had one baby daughter, but both father and child died of influenza. As in her sister's case, Kate's husband's Tlingit clan wanted her to remain on the coast so they could arrange an appropriate second marriage. But by now, her mother back in Carcross was so deeply distressed by the loss of her daughters that she insisted Kate return. The startling number of deaths was forcing people to improvise in cases where remarriage of widows was concerned: a fourth sister had recently married a white prospector/trader named George Carmack, but she too had died from the influenza that was ravaging interior communities by now. Kate's mother insisted that it was more appropriate for Kate to return to the interior to marry her deceased sister's husband than to remain on the coast. Partnerships between brothers-in-law were very important, and with Carmack's second marriage into the family, he and Skookum Jim became strong allies. But shortly after this, Carmack and Kate followed her sister downriver where rumors of gold were attracting prospectors.

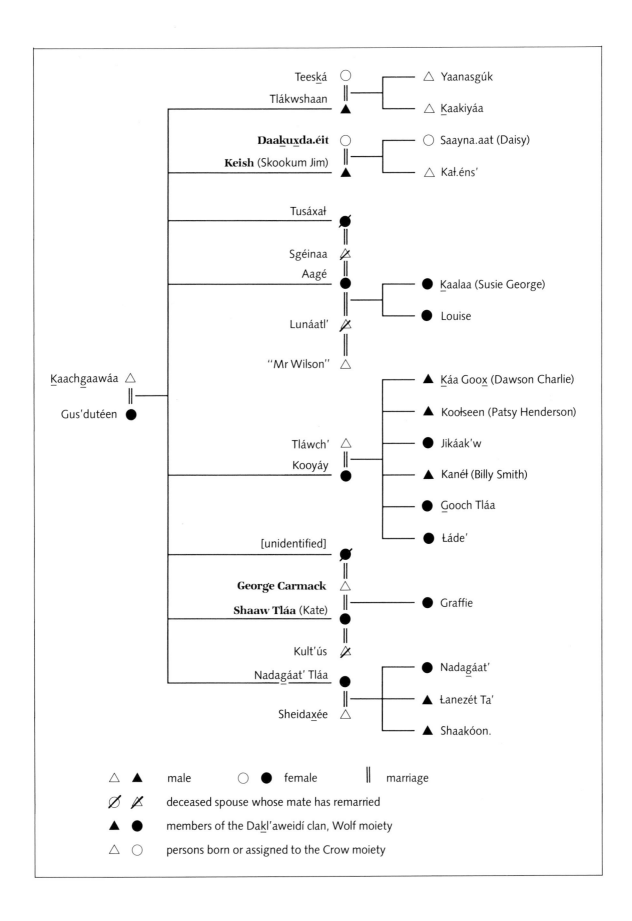

Teeská ○
Tlákwshaan ▲ ───┬─── △ Yaanasgúk
                 └─── △ Ḵaakiyáa

Daaḵuxda.éit ○
Keish (Skookum Jim) ▲ ───┬─── ○ Saayna.aat (Daisy)
                         └─── △ Kaɫ.éns'

Tusáxaɫ ⊘

Sgéinaa ⌀
Aagé ● ───┬─── ● Ḵaalaa (Susie George)
          └─── ● Louise

Lunáatl' ⌀

"Mr Wilson" △
                      ┌─── ▲ Ḵáa Goox (Dawson Charlie)
                      ├─── ▲ Kooɫseen (Patsy Henderson)
                      ├─── ● Jikáak'w
Kaachgaawáa △
Gus'dutéen ●

Tláwch' △
Kooyáy ● ───┼─── ▲ Kanéɫ (Billy Smith)
            ├─── ● Gooch Tláa
            └─── ● Ɫáde'

[unidentified] ⊘

George Carmack △
Shaaw Tláa (Kate) ● ─── ● Graffie

Kult'ús ⌀

Nadagáat' Tláa ● ───┬─── ● Nadagáat'
                    ├─── ▲ Ɫanezét Ta'
Sheidaxée △   └─── ▲ Shaaḵóon.

△ ▲ male   ○ ● female   ‖ marriage

⊘ ⌀ deceased spouse whose mate has remarried

▲ ● members of the Daḵl'aweidí clan, Wolf moiety

△ ○ persons born or assigned to the Crow moiety

130

Still another of Skookum Jim's sisters, Nadagaat' Tláa, died a tragic death when she and her daughter were caught in an unexpected winter storm on a mountain pass as they returned to Carcross over the Chilkoot Pass. Only one sister, Kooyáy, remained with her parents, married in a customary alliance in the interior. She raised a large family, including the nephews who later accompanied Keish on his travels downriver.

In a very few years, then, Keish lost one brother and three sisters. Of the surviving three sisters, two had gone "down the river" with white husbands, leaving only one sister still living safely at home. Elders insist that Skookum Jim was *not* prospecting with Carmack in 1896. Instead, they say, he was living on the southern lakes, preoccupied with the whereabouts of his two sisters.

Mrs Sidney begins her account:

In the first place, he wasn't looking for gold.
Skookum Jim went downriver to look for his two sisters,
because [people] missed them.
They were gone two years already – no telegram, nothing!
He didn't know whether his two sisters were alive or not.
That's why he thought he'd go down the river too,
to see if he could find his sisters, Aagé and Kate.
They were strict about that kind of thing, old people.

She goes on to describe how a party was selected to go, who was chosen, who stayed behind, and why. Her own parents went part way, as far as Lake Laberge, but turned back when they considered how difficult it would be for their elderly family members to survive the winter if they were delayed.

[Skookum Jim] took his wife and his two nephews –
Dawson Charlie and Patsy Henderson.
My father was going too, but they turned back at Lake Laberge.
My father turned to my mother and he said [looking back at the
*   mountain behind Carcross]*
"See that Chílíh Dzéle'?" And she started to cry.
"Why are you crying?"
"I'm just thinking about your poor crippled mother, and your sister
*   and my mother.*
Who is going to cut wood for them?
Who is going to help them get water?
They're sick and crippled and helpless."
And so my father and mother turned around and went back –
Otherwise they might have found the gold too.
Bad luck, eh?
But maybe it was just as well. . . .
All those men who found gold split up with their wives. . . .

Mrs Smith's husband, Billy (Keneł'), was one of the young men who was left behind to look after his mother, Kooyáy. Mrs Smith heard the story many times after her marriage, from the perspective of Kate, who was living in Carcross by then:

Mrs Lucy Wren, granddaughter of Nadagaat' Tláa, has recorded her grandmother's story on tape. A transcript is available in the Curriculum Development Branch of the Council for Yukon Indians.

131

Keish's sister Shaaw Tláa (Kate
Carmack). *Yukon Archives.*

Skookum Jim worries about his sister, you know,
"Oh, my. Going to get lost.
Don't want to get lost, my sister."
That's what he says: he talks about it all winter.
Dawson Charlie tells him,
"I guess we go down to look for her.
We're going to bring her back," he tells his uncle.
Kate Carmack tells me all that.
They just go look for her.
They're not looking for gold!

Her account attributes the overall success of the party to Kate's skills and to those of other women they met:

They live one winter, Kate Carmack and him, her husband.
He's got wife.
He's all right!
She does everything, that Indian woman, you know —
hunts, just like nothing,
sets snares for rabbits.
That's what they eat.
I know her: that's my auntie, Kate Carmack,
my old man's mother's sister.
One lady, Dawson people, gave them fish.
She cut it up, Kate Carmack —
that's how they lived all winter....

In Mrs Smith's version of the story, the actual discovery of the gold is secondary to Skookum Jim's journey downriver to find his missing sisters. This pattern of a hero who uses all his powers to undertake a journey to find his wife or sisters is an important one in narratives from the southern Yukon, and occurs in many of the old stories.

Stories of the aftermath of the gold rush focus on the close connection between wealth and tragedy. Carried away by their unexpected fortune, the men became involved in a lifestyle that cost each of them his family. Keish's wife left him and returned to her coastal Tlingit family. Her parents were disturbed by their daughter's violation of custom and they brought her back to her husband in Carcross, but Keish no longer seemed to care. She left again, taking their son while Keish kept their daughter Daisy.

Dawson Charlie's wife, Sadusgé, left too. Alcohol played a part in his accidental death a few years later.

Kate returned to Carcross alone, abandoned by George who virtually kidnapped their daughter, Graffie, taking her south with him. Graffie's removal from the community was particularly devastating in a culture where a child belongs to her mother's clan, and is still deeply troubling to elders who discuss it. Kate died in 1920 at the age of 63, during the worldwide influenza epidemic. In the seventy years since her death, the story of the Klondike gold rush has been told in print many

A similar account comes from Patsy Henderson, who was another of Skookum Jim's nephews and Dawson Charlie's younger brother. He was the youngest member of the party, though his name rarely appears in written accounts. His Tagish name was Koołseen and his English name was given to him by George Carmack. Years later, he used to give public lectures, describing how he remembered the event. He explained that he was "just a kid" when he made the journey downriver with his uncle, looking for his aunt and her husband. (One of Patsy Henderson's lectures was recorded and transcribed in 1949 and is part of the Yukon Archives pamphlet collection under the title "Early Days at Caribou Crossing: The Discovery of Gold on the Klondike.")

Johnny Johns tells how Keish's nephew Yaanasgúk came back to Carcross to visit his uncle's and father's country years later. While in Carcross, he made up a Tlingit song for his uncle's and father's Dakl'aweidí kinsmen:

Oh, it makes my heart feel bad,
this my father's country.
It's alright if I do die
in this, my father's country.

Johnny Johns told this story and recorded the song. The recording is on file with the Curriculum Development Program, Council for Yukon Indians.

times. But Kate scarcely appears in written accounts of these events in which she was such a central player.

Skookum Jim's daughter, Daisy, studied acting briefly in California and made periodic trips back to Carcross, particularly when her father was ill. She was uncertain, though, about how she could fit into Carcross life. She had grown up without any of the skills every Tagish woman would have learned. She once told Mrs Sidney that she would like to marry and stay in Carcross, but it seemed that no man of the appropriate clan would have her. "She's too much white lady. Who wants to marry a white lady?" one prospective candidate told Mrs Sidney. After her father's death in 1916, Daisy left, married, divorced, and remarried but her life was not a happy one. Her health deteriorated rapidly. According to papers filed with her father's lawyers, she died in 1938 at the age of 47.

One aspect of the written record may seem minor, but it is particularly troubling to elders. Both Skookum Jim and the nephews who accompanied him were members of the Dakl'aweidí clan. One of these nephews, Káa Goox, earned the English name Dawson Charlie because of his adventures near the place named Dawson City at the time of the gold rush. In written accounts, though, his is usually referred to as "Tagish Charlie" because whites identified him as a Tagish man who came from Tagish Lake. The naming causes confusion because a different man, whose name was Yéił Saagí, was known in the southern Yukon as Tagish Charlie. This man was a prominent member of the Deisheetaan clan and was not involved in the discovery. In Chapter 4, the significance of clan ownership of names was discussed. To emphasize her concern about the importance of getting names correct, Mrs Sidney points to the two graves of men in the Carcross cemetery, Tagish Charlie (Yéił Saagí) with his Deisheetaan (Beaver) crest on his stone, and Dawson Charlie (Káa Goox) with his Dakl'aweidí (Wolf) crest on his.

Gold rush stories persist in the Yukon because they appeal to popular imagination. Part of their appeal comes from the ideas about social organization implied by these stories. The question of which version is "correct" may not be as interesting or useful as the question, what does each version reveal about the different cultural values of its narrators?

Written accounts of the gold rush portray Skookum Jim as an idealized frontiersman – a rather one-dimensional character, "an Indian who wanted to be a white man," and a lone prospector whose efforts are ultimately rewarded. This model would have been important to many of the prospectors who travelled north because it expressed their own hopes. Many of them would have read or heard the immensely popular stories written by Horatio Alger during the latter part of the century. In Alger's stories, characters always succeeded by their own efforts in spite of poverty and deprivation. Horatio Alger wrote 120 books and those books sold over twenty million copies, making him one of the most successful writers of his day. Skookum Jim, as he is portrayed in written accounts, could easily have been a hero in one of Alger's books.

Oral accounts from his own community belong to a different tradition of narrative. In southern Yukon storytelling, many stories that have a man as the central character dramatize a journey he makes with the assistance of an animal helper. In the course of the journey, the hero has experiences which enable him to understand the world in a new and different way. If fortunate, he is able to bring that knowledge back to the community so that it benefits everyone. Many people suggest that while Skookum Jim followed the advice of his Frog helper carefully, his final days would have been happier had he also paid closer attention to Tl'anaxéedakw.

People who knew Keish also describe him as a man strongly influenced by social and cultural customs important in his community. His concern about his sisters' whereabouts is entirely understandable to elders: his sister and her children were members of his clan, not the clan of her husband or their father, so he was ultimately responsible for them. In his journey down the Yukon, he was not only following the guidance of Frog, he was also carrying out his responsibilities as the senior surviving brother in his family.

In both the written and oral records, then, Skookum Jim exhibits the qualities of an "ideal man," even if those ideals differ according to the cultural values of the teller. Written accounts idealize the image of the lone prospector and adventurer. Oral accounts stress that he was a committed Dakl'aweidí clan member who followed the guidance of his spirit helper. The stories differ partly because each ideal reflects a very different view of society, and these differences were to become even more apparent with the cultural clashes of the twentieth century.

Maybe, after all, oral tradition teaches us more about differences in cultural values, in attitudes, and interpretation than it teaches about events. Ultimately, the question becomes whether Yukon society is one in which people are expected to succeed on individual merit, following a western model, or whether ideas about success are more firmly embedded in family and community. These stories persist because they say something important about goals in present-day society, even if those goals may be conflicting.

The opportunities for seeing such different perspectives increase now that written records can be combined with oral memories, bringing a range of voices to discussions about the Yukon's past and present.

Shaaw Tláa (Kate Carmack) in later life, at Carcross. *Anglican Church of Canada, General Synod Archives.*

Angela Sidney

To start with, Skookum Jim's family built a house there in Dyea.
People used to go there long time ago before Dyea was a city.
They had only one store there.
They stayed there all the time, Skookum Jim's family.
In fall time, the ground is getting frozen already.
But it's coast, you know, that different climate.

Here, he went to bathroom outside.
When he's coming back, he hears something making a noise.
"Whoo . . ." – just like sand pouring down.
So he stopped and listened.
Here there was a ditch alongside the house where they dug up the
     sand and put it on the moss for roofing.
That's what they used, long time ago.

So he went to the edge and he looked down.
Sure enough there was a big frog – coast frogs are bigger than these
     frogs, you know.
Long way from water, too, they said.
Here it was trying to jump up and trying to get back but it fell down.
Kept doing that, I don't know how long.
Gravel fell down with him – that's what's making the noise.

Anyway, Skookum Jim saw it, so he looked around for a board.
Here he found a board and he shoved it down that hole
and then that frog crawled on that board.

So Uncle Skookum Jim lifted it up.
He lifted it up and carried it and took it down to the creek –
there must be a creek there – this is Dyea.
So anyway, he left it there.
He let it go.

And about a year or so after,
here he got kicked in the stomach by a drunkard man.
And it got festered – oh, he was sick, they say.
It happened somewhere around wintertime.
He was so sick he couldn't move anymore.
And here that sickness broke open to the outside.

That's when my mother was looking after him.
Well, he's my Daddy's cousin – their mothers were sisters.
My mother's got three kids – four altogether with my oldest brother.
And my mother's got one baby and twin girls, four altogether.
She was looking after them.

Skookum Jim's wife and my Daddy,
they go back, pack stuff [for prospectors].
They're freighting over the summit toward Bennett.
They get paid for packing stuff: flour, soap, everything like that.
And that's what my father was doing.
My mother stayed home and looked after the kids and my uncle,
        Skookum Jim.

Here one morning in June, his stomach broke out.
Sun was way out already when my mother heard Skookum Jim calling
        her:
"Mrs John, Mrs John, Ła.oos Tláa, Ła.oos Tláa,
wake up. Come on."

Well, she got up – she's a young person.
She jumped up and went over there.
"Look at this thing here!"
Well, he was too hot – it was just burning, that sore place.
So he had his blanket way up and his shirt way open,
and he pulled off those bandages because it was too hot.
He wanted to air it, that open place.

And here he feels something tickling him there –
that's why he looked down.
Here it was a frog licking that sore place.
That's what it was that woke him up.
My mother saw it and then she just got a board or something and put
        the frog on that.
It never jumped too, nothing, just stayed like that.

Well, my mother used to have silk thread and beads and stuff too. She
        was good then – she wasn't blind then.
They gave that frog silk thread and some beads.
They put swan down feathers all around him too.
Then she took it down to the creek and left it there.
That's payment for Skookum Jim to that frog.
They paid him.

And here two or three days after, he started feeling better,
and that started healing up, too.
So it healed up good in no time – just in a week or so.
He's all better and he's able to walk around good again.

I don't know how long after that he wants to see his mother –
his mother lives in Carcross.
Naataase Héen they call it in Tlingit,
        "Water running through the narrows."
Tagish language they call it *Todezaane*,
        "Blowing all the time."
He wants to see if his mother is okay.
It's getting to be fall time –
the ground is frozen already, but no snow yet.

So he went through the pass here [route of present Tagish road]
Shásh Zéitígí, "grizzly bear throat," they call it.
They call it that because north wind's always blowing through —
it's open there, too, just like down a throat.

Through there, he went to see his mother, down in Carcross.
And here he camped half way around the first lake [Crag Lake],
just right in the middle.
There's a camp place there all the time — brush camp —
and here he camped there.
He slept there.

That's the time he dreamed nice looking lady came to him —
gee, she's just pure — just like you can see through her,
just like shining, gold shining.

He said that lady told him
"I come for you,
I want you to come with me.
I come for you now.
I want you to marry me," she said.

And my uncle said,
"No, I can't marry you.
I got wife already.
My wife and children are in Tagish."
That's what he dreamed he told this lady, he said.

"Well," she said,
"If you can't go with me, I'll give you my walking stick."
So he took it.
He tells her, "Thank you."

"You saved me one time," she said.
"I was almost starving and I was just about going to die.
And here you saved me one time.
And I'm the one that saved you too when you were sick.
When you were sick, I saved you.
I helped you.
I medicined you.
That's why you got better."
That's what that lady's supposed to tell him because he dreamed that.

And that lady told him when she gave him that walking stick:
"You're going to find the bottom of this walking stick.
You're going to find it this way."
So he looked at it, and gee, everything is shining, looks like gold.
"Look this way," she said, pointing to Atlin, "Look this way."
He looks and sees just like a search light coming up.
"That's not for you though; that's for somebody else.
You go down this way and you're going to have your luck,
your walking stick," [indicating down the Yukon River].
That's what that lady is supposed to tell him.

When he woke up in the morning,
here there was snow on top of him, about a foot deep, they say.
It snowed that night.
I guess he slept in an open place.
He didn't sleep under anything.

After he ate breakfast, he went down to Carcross.
He went to Carcross that night.
And his mother and those people are all fine.
It's all okay.
That's after his father died, I suppose — they never mention his father
      when they tell this story — they just say his mother.
Some of her grandchildren are staying with them.
She was fine — nothing wrong — lots of wood — lots to eat.
Everything.

So he just stayed one night, and then he started back.
He camped on the way back too.
Then finally he got home.
He thought he was gone four days.

When he got there they tell him,
"What kept you so long?
You've been gone eleven days."

Well after that he forgot about his dream.
About a year later, though,
that's the time he went down Yukon River.
He didn't think any more about it
until he went down the river and found gold.

_____

Mrs Annie Ned, about 1988. *Photo by Julie Cruikshank.*

Varieties of History 8

IN NORTHERN CANADA, it is frequently possible to hear contrasting interpretations of landscape, life experiences, or events from the past. Some of these accounts are recorded in written records; others are part of the daily conversation of elders. History books have usually taken their evidence about the past from written records. Until recently, oral testimonies have often been lumped together as "anecdotal" accounts, the very term suggesting that they lack a serious purpose.

Interest in what can be learned from oral accounts is growing, particularly in North and South America, in Africa, and in the South Pacific – all parts of the world where oral and written sources are likely to interpret events in different ways. But oral tradition seems to give us an opportunity to learn more than simply new facts. Frequently, orally narrated accounts actually challenge historians' ideas about what a "fact" really is.

Stories are far more than just accounts of events. They are also statements of worldview. They encompass many layers of meaning. Considerable thought is given to the question of when a young person is ready to hear a particular narrative, who should tell it, whether the youngster is capable of understanding the embedded messages. One point adults frequently make when they talk about their *own* education is how stories build up layers of significance as one grows older. Stories heard at different stages of life – in childhood, at times of transition, and in adulthood – carry different meanings each time. The link between storyteller and student becomes critical.

The term *oral tradition*, then, is often used to refer to two different things. Sometimes we use it to point to a body of *material* retained from the past and known to elders. Other times, we use the term to talk about a *process* by which that material has been handed down to the present. Both of these aspects are important, but definitions like this may make oral tradition seem more rigid than it really is. Oral tradition is more than a body of stories to be recorded and stored away, and it is not always passed on in the form of complete narratives. Anyone who has spent time talking with elders about their understanding of the past knows that oral accounts are discussed and debated in communities, and that oral tradition itself is a lively, continuous, ongoing process, a way of understanding the present as well as the past.

In the preceding chapters, we have looked at ways in which our understandings of the world are constructed. This book covers a period of time beginning in the distant past and ending with the gold

"History" is about how we make chronicles. How we manipulate facts. How we exploit and shape and bend memory. How we make up stories to make sense of our past.
– *Granta*, Vol. 32, 1990

History is to be learned from, not lived in.
– Council for Yukon Indians, *Together Today for our Children Tomorrow* (1977), p 9

rush, but the questions it raises continue to be even more important during this century.

Like any system of knowledge, oral tradition has particular goals, methods, and questions, but they differ from those of Euramerican science or history. Beginning with different questions, oral tradition, science and history provide us with different, but equally valuable, ways of understanding relationships among environment, animals and humans. Because translation is such an imperfect process, it may be that cultural outsiders can best begin by trying to understand the *questions* raised by oral tradition rather than trying to extract quick answers or "facts" from it.

In some ways, oral and scientific traditions are clearly distinct. There are areas, though, where it seems particularly important to bring them together. Combining the two traditions may help us to learn how human ideas and human behaviour influence and are influenced by the environment. People have been living in the north since at least the last glaciation, and possibly longer. Hunting peoples do not simply react passively to their environment, they also work actively with it. Their long-term survival has depended on their awareness and understanding of the complex relationships among landscape, climate, vegetation and animals. As we become more aware on a worldwide scale of the critical need to maintain balances and not deplete resources, indigenous knowledge may play a special role in helping science catch up to these problems.

A good example of how oral and scientific traditions explore different questions concerns the peopling of North America, discussed in Chapter 3. Archaeologists are interested in the question of when and how people came to populate North and South America. The evidence they use comes from physical remains or by-products of human activity. Elders are less concerned with *where* people came from than with the broader question of *how* people came to be fully human. They tell narratives about how the world originated and how it was transformed to make it a place suitable for people to live. Once the framework is expanded to include both kinds of questions, there is room for both kinds of answers as well

The European historical and scientific tradition encourages us to remember the names of particular people – scientists, scholars, statesmen – long after they are dead. But there is every reason to believe that thinkers of Albert Einstein's calibre have been present in all populations in all periods of history. We might think about this by visualizing human knowledge as a kind of giant pie, with different pieces representing different subjects from among the many topics available in the world. Each society emphasizes the sectors or pieces that they come to consider most important. Those judgements differ from culture to culture and from one period of history to another. For example, during the last hundred years, European and American cultures have paid a lot of attention to a sector that we call science and technology. Native American cultures have generally concerned themselves with other problems, like kinship and the relationships between people, as

Tommy McGinty and Stanley Jonathan (above) and John Dickson (below) at the Northern Storytelling Festival, 1990. *Yukon Government photos.*

well as relationships between humans, other animals, and the land. Both traditions are complex. Both pose difficult questions that require intellectual effort for a full understanding of the issues involved. But that effort may take different forms.

Subarctic hunting cultures value a kind of intellectual achievement demonstrated by the ability to learn, remember and pass on the understandings embedded in oral tradition. In literate cultures, the tradition can come to seem very impersonal. Reading and writing are solitary activities, and the written word may seem to come from a source remote in space or time. But in cultures where essential knowledge is passed on by word of mouth, everything saved from the past is heard in a living voice. No matter how old the story, it will be interpreted and transmitted by someone close at hand. This changes our perception of the story and our relationship to it. It also changes our perception of time itself, and our relationship to time.

One example, which we have already discussed in some detail, is the fur trade. History books may treat the fur trade as a particular event or period in Canadian history, but for northern Native peoples, trapping for trade began long before Canada was a country and continues to be important today. It represents a way of life instead of a period of time with a beginning and an end.

Like oral accounts, written records express a point of view. That point of view is shaped by the cultural traditions and the experiences of those who make the records. Fur traders, missionaries, scientists and prospectors who came to the Yukon during the second half of the nineteenth century were influenced by their own distinct cultural traditions and brought definite perspectives to their observations about aboriginal people in the north. The most striking thing about these accounts is that they are testimonies to the personalities and cultures of their writers and pay little or no attention to the perspectives of the people they were describing. Scottish traders were leaving impoverished farms. English missionaries trained in strict Victorian schools were leaving a rigid class system. American scientists from the eastern United States were eager to combine science with the idea of exploration. Prospectors were propelled north by a worldwide depression and a taste for adventure. These were among the early representatives of "western culture" to come to the Yukon. One theme that seems to emerge from accounts of early visitors is their commitment to the idea of collection. Furs, souls, "facts," precious metals and pieces of real estate were collected. Big-game hunters still come to the north collecting trophies in much the same way. Knowing something about the backgrounds from which these collectors have come may make their activities more understandable. At the same time, it clarifies the cultural contrasts that existed between early European and Euramerican visitors to the Yukon, on one hand, and Athapaskan and Tlingit residents, on the other.

Such differences in understanding are perhaps clearest when we look at specific examples, like the one from the Klondike gold rush, discussed in Chapter 7. Instead of focussing on the "truth" or "accuracy" of different accounts of the gold rush, it is worth looking at the

narrative customs shaping both written and oral accounts. Both are shaped by the cultural values of their tellers. The oral accounts of Native elders and the written accounts of visitors contrast so starkly because they reflect different ideas about how society should be organized. Prospectors saw the Yukon as a frontier where everything they found was theirs. Athapaskan and Tlingit residents knew it as their homeland. Looking at the stories that influenced those narrators helps us to understand both kinds of accounts. The contribution of oral tradition to written history may not consist so much of new facts. Its most important contribution may consist of new questions, perspectives, and interpretations.

As the Yukon enters the 1990s, increasing attention is being paid to indigenous perspectives on the past, and the oral accounts of elders have at last begun to reach a wider audience. At the annual Northern Storytelling Festival, held in Whitehorse, elders such as Tommy McGinty, Stanley Jonathon, Annie Ned, John Dickson and Angela Sidney tell stories to crowds of attentive listeners. Northern Native Broadcasting has produced videotaped documentaries on historical and contemporary issues, and these are being transmitted across northern Canada on television. The Yukon Heritage and Museums Association has sponsored several conferences on themes where both elders and academics participate and exchange ideas about topics that interest all of them. The Heritage Branch of the Territorial Government has funded individual First Nations in the Yukon to conduct their own oral history projects. The Yukon Native Language Centre continues to document languages, narratives and history in indigenous languages, and to ensure that these become part of the regular school program throughout the Territory. The Curriculum Development Program of the Council for Yukon Indians is developing community-based curriculum for use in Yukon classrooms. Together, these projects are helping to ensure that the cultural heritage of First Nations is seen not simply as part of the past, but as a continuing and growing force in the Yukon's present and future.

The endurance of oral tradition in the Yukon speaks directly to the strength and flexibility of Athapaskan and Tlingit ways of life. Recognition of debts to old tradition is indispensable to the creation of new tradition. Through this process, First Nations in the Yukon are demonstrating the tremendous importance of storytelling in helping to sustain cultures undergoing rapid and dislocating change.

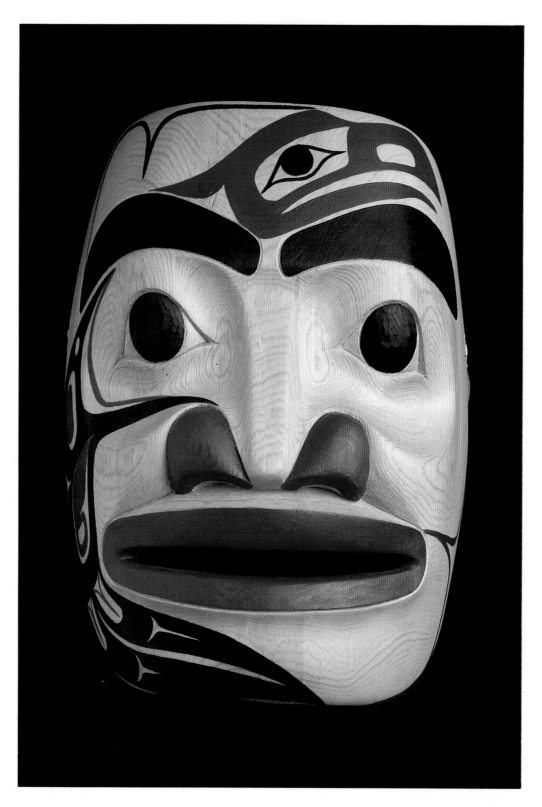

The face of *Àjanà Zhaya*, by Kitty Smith
(opposite) and a Crow mask (above) by
Mark Porter of Teslin. *Yukon
Government photos.*

Bibliography

Adney, Tappan
    1900   *The Klondike Stampede.* New York and London: Harper and Brothers.

    1900   Moose hunting with the Tro-chu-tin. *Harper's New Monthly Magazine* 100(597): 495–507.

    1902   The Indian Hunter of the Far Northwest. *Outing* 39(6): 623–33.

Berton, Pierre
    1958   *Klondike: The Life and Death of the Last Great Gold Rush.* Toronto: McClelland & Stewart.

Binney, Judith
    1987   Maori Oral Narratives and Pakeha Written Texts: Two Forms of Telling History. *New Zealand Journal of History* 21(1): 16–28.

Bird, J. Brian
    1972   The Physical Characteristics of Northern Canada. In: William C. Wonders, ed. *The North.* Toronto: University of Toronto Press.

Bostock, Hugh S.
    1969   Kluane Lake, Yukon Territory: Its Drainage and Allied Problems. Ottawa: Geological Survey of Canada. Paper No. 69-28.

Bronowski, Jacob
    1977   *A Sense of the Future.* Cambridge, Mass.: M.I.T. Press.

Campbell, Robert
    1958   *Two Journals of Robert Campbell, 1808–1853.* Edited by J.W. Todd, Jr. Seattle: J.W. Todd Jr. Ltd.

Champagne-Aishihik Band & Sha-tan Tours
    1988   *From Trail to Highway: Kwädāy kwätän ts'än ek'än tān ksätsin.* Whitehorse.

Coates, Ken
    1980   Furs Along the Yukon: Hudson's Bay Company – Native Trade in the Yukon River Basin, 1830–1893. Master's Thesis, Department of History, University of Manitoba.

Council for Yukon Indians
    1977   *Together Today for Our Children Tomorrow.* Whitehorse: Council for Yukon Indians.

Cressman, L.S.
    1977   *Prehistory of the Far West: Homes of Vanished People.* Salt Lake City: University of Utah Press.

Cruikshank, Julie
    1978   *When the World Began.* Whitehorse: Government of Yukon, Department of Education.

    1981   Legend and Landscape: Convergence of Oral and Scientific Traditions in the Yukon Territory. *Arctic Anthropology* 18(2): 67–93.

1989   Oral Tradition and Written Accounts: An Incident from the Klondike Gold Rush. *Culture* 9(2): 1–10.

1990   Getting the Words Right: Perspectives on Naming and Places in Athapaskan Oral History. *Arctic Anthropology* 27(1): 52–65.

Cruikshank, Julie, in collaboration with Angela Sidney, Kitty Smith & Annie Ned
1990   *Life Lived Like a Story: Life Stories of Three Yukon Elders.* Lincoln: University of Nebraska Press; Vancouver: University of British Columbia Press.

Dall, William H.
1870   *Alaska and Its Resources.* Boston: Lee & Shepard.

Davidson, George
1901   Explanation of an Indian Map of the Rivers, Lakes, Trails and Mountains from the Chilkaht to the Yukon drawn by the Chilkaht Chief, Kohklux, in 1869. *Mazama,* April 1901: 75–82.

Dawson, George
1888   Notes on the Indian Tribes of the Yukon District and Adjacent Northern Portion of British Columbia, 1887. *Annual Report of the Geological Survey of Canada,* n.s. 3(2): 191B–213B.

1898   *Report on an Exploration in the Yukon District, Northwest Territories and Adjacent Northern Portion of British Columbia, 1887.* Ottawa: Geological Survey of Canada.

De Laguna, Frederica
1972   *Under Mount St Elias: The History and Culture of the Yakutat Tlingit.* Smithsonian Contributions to Anthropology No. 7, 3 vols. Washington, D.C.

Duchaussois, P.
1923   *Mid Snow and Ice: The Apostles of the Northwest.* London: Burns, Oates & Washbourne.

Duncan, Kate
1989   *Northern Athapaskan Art: A Beadwork Tradition.* Seattle: University of Washington Press.

Fagan, Brian
1989   *People of the Earth: An Introduction to World Prehistory,* 6th edition. Glenview, Ill.: Scott, Foresman/Little, Brown.

Field, Poole
1957   The Poole Field Letters, 1913. Edited by June Helm MacNeish. *Anthropologica* 4: 47–60.

Fredson, John
1982   *John Fredson Edward Sapir Hàa Googwandak: Stories Told by John Fredson to Edward Sapir.* Edited by Katherine Peter and Jane McGary. Fairbanks: Alaska Native Language Center.

Glave, Edward J.
1890–1 Our Alaska Expedition. In: *Frank Leslie's Illustrated newspaper.* 28 June, 12 July, 19 July, 9 August, 16 August, 6 September, 15 November, 22 November, 29 November, 6 December, 13 December, 20 December, 27 December, 1890; 3 January, 10 January, 1891.

Gould, Stephen Jay
1989   *Wonderful Life: The Burgess Shale and the Nature of History.* New York: W.W. Norton.

Granta
1990   History. *Granta* 32. Cambridge, England.

Habgood, Thelma
1970   Indian Legends of Northwestern Canada, by Emile Petitot. *Western Canadian Journal of Anthropology* 2(1): 94–129.

Henderson, Patsy
1950   Early Days at Caribou Crossing: The Discovery of Gold on the Klondike. Recorded by Jennie Mae Moyer. Unpublished manuscript, Yukon Archives pamphlet collection.

Jarvis, A.M.
1899   Annual Report of Inspector A.M. Jarvis, 1898. Ottawa: *Annual Report of the North-west Mounted Police,* 1899: 95–110.

Keele, Joseph
1957   Reconnaissance Across the Mackenzie Mountains on the Pelly, Ross and Gravel Rivers, 1907–08. In: H.S. Bostock, ed. *Yukon Territory. Selected Field Reports of the Geological Survey of Canada, 1898–1933,* Memoir 284: 283–314.

King, A. Richard
1967   *The School at Mopass.* New York: Holt Rinehart and Winston.

Krause, Aurel
1956   *The Tlingit Indians.* Erna Gunther, trans. Seattle: University of Washington Press. (Originally published 1885.)

Kruger, Barbara, and Phil Mariani
1989   *Remaking History.* Dia Art Foundation. Discussions in Contemporary Culture No. 4. Seattle: Bay Press.

McCandless, Robert
1985   *Yukon Wildlife.* Edmonton: University of Alberta Press.

McClellan, Catharine
1950   Culture Change and Native Trade in the Southern Yukon Territory. PhD Dissertation.,Department of Anthropology, University of California, Berkeley.

1963   Wealth Woman and Frogs among the Tagish Indians. *Anthropos* 58: 121–8.

1975   *My Old People Say: An Ethnographic Survey of the Southern Yukon Territory.* National Museum of Canada Publications in Ethnology 6, 2 vols. Ottawa.

1970   Indian Stories about the First Whites in Northwestern America. In: Margaret Lantis, ed. *Ethnohistory in Southwestern Alaska and the Southern Yukon: Method and Content.* Lexington: University Press of Kentucky.

McClellan, Catharine, with Lucie Birckel, Robert Bringhurst, James A. Fall, Carol McCarthy & Janice Sheppard
1987   *Part of the Land, Part of the Water: A History of the Yukon Indians.* Vancouver and Toronto: Douglas & McIntyre.

McConnell, R.G.
1891   *Report on an Exploration in the Yukon and Mackenzie Basins, N.W.T.* Montreal: William Foster Brown.

McDonnell, Roger
1975   Kasini Society: Some Aspects of the Social Organization of an Athapaskan Culture Between 1900–1950. PhD Dissertation, University of British Columbia.

Murray, Alexander Hunter
1910   *Journal of the Yukon, 1847–8.* Ottawa: Government Printing Office.

Northern Native Broadcasting
1988   *The Mission School Syndrome.* Whitehorse: Northern Native Broadcasting.

1990   *Old Crow: A Documentary.* Whitehorse: Northern Native Broadcasting.

Ned, Annie
1984   *Old People in Those Days, They Told Their Story All the Time.*
Whitehorse: Yukon Native Languages Project.

Ogilvie, William
1913   *Early Days on the Yukon.* Ottawa: Thornburn & Abbott.

Osgood, Cornelius
1970   *Contributions to the Ethnography of the Kutchin.* New Haven: Human
Relations Area Files.

Sahlins, Marshall
1985   *Islands of History.* Chicago: University of Chicago Press.

Schwatka, Frederick
1898   *Along Alaska's Great River.* Chicago: Henry.

Sidney, Angela
1980   *Place Names of the Tagish Region, Southern Yukon.* Whitehorse: Yukon
Native Languages Project.

1982   *Tagish Tlaagú/Tagish Stories.* Recorded by Julie Cruikshank. Whitehorse:
Council for Yukon Indians and the Government of Yukon.

1983   *Haa Shagóon.* Compiled by Julie Cruikshank. Whitehorse: Yukon Native
Languages Project.

Sidney, Angela, Kitty Smith & Rachel Dawson
1977   *My Stories Are My Wealth.* As told to Julie Cruikshank. Whitehorse:
Council for Yukon Indians

Simon, Sarah
1982   *Fort McPherson, N.W.T.: A Pictorial Account of Family, Church, and
Community.* Whitehorse: Council for Yukon Indians and Government of
Yukon.

Slobodin, Richard
1962   *Band Organization of the Peel River Kutchin.* National Museum of Canada
Bulletin 179. Ottawa.

1963   'The Dawson Boys' – Peel River Indians and the Dawson Gold Rush. *Polar
Record* 5: 24–35.

Smith, Kitty
1982   *Nindal Kwädindür/I'm Going to Tell you a Story.* Recorded by Julie
Cruikshank. Whitehorse: Council for Yukon Indians and Government of
Yukon.

Strommel, Henry & Elizabeth Strommel
1979   The Year Without a Summer. *Scientific American* 240(6): 134–140.

Swanton, John
1909   *Tlingit Myths and Texts.* Bureau of American Ethnology Bulletin 39.
Washington, D.C.

Tanner, Adrian
1965   The Structure of Fur Trade Relations. Master's thesis, Department of
Anthropology, University of British Columbia.

Tarbuck, Edward J. & Frederick K. Lutgens
  1987   *The Earth: An Introduction to Physical Geology.* Columbus, Ohio: Merrill
         Publishing Company.

Teit, James
  1917   Kaska Tales. *Journal of American Folklore* 30(118): 427–473.

Tien, Daniel L.
  1986   *Speaking Out: Consultations and Survey of Yukon Native Languages
         Planning, Visibility and Growth.* Whitehorse: Yukon Native Language
         Centre.

Tom, Gertie
  1981   *Dùts'ūm Edhó Ts'ètsi Yū Dän K'í: How to Tan Hides in the Native Way.*
         Whitehorse: Yukon Native Languages Project.

  1987   *Èkeyi: Gyò Cho Chú: My Country, Big Salmon River.* Whitehorse: Yukon
         Native Language Centre.

Vansina, Jan.
  1971   Once Upon a Time: Oral Traditions as History in Africa. *Daedalus* 100(2):
         442–468.

Wahl, H.E., D.B. Fraser, R.C. Harvey, & J.B. Maxwell
  1987   *Climate of the Yukon.* Climatological Studies No. 40. Ottawa: Environment
         Canada.

Workman, William
  1978   *Prehistory of the Aishihik-Kluane Area, Southwest Yukon Territory.*
         Archeological Survey of Canada, Paper No. 74, Mercury Series, Ottawa:
         National Museums of Canada.

Wright, Al
  1976   *Prelude to Bonanza.* Sidney, British Columbia: Gray's Publishing.

Index

The alphabets used for writing Tlingit and Athapaskan languages include modified versions of several roman letters. In these alphabets, K, K̲, K' represent three different sounds and are therefore different letters. L and Ł are also separate letters. So are T, T', Tl and Tl'. Each of these should therefore have its own place in the alphabet, but that means learning a new alphabetical order to look up words. Here, for the convenience of people who have not yet mastered these writing systems, we have treated K, K̲ and K' as if they were the same, and we have treated the letter Tl as if it were T plus L, instead of a separate letter of its own.

D1284296